¡FOODIE!

BELGIAN BEERS

Beer Sommelier Ben Vinken

photography by Joris Luyten

dedicated to Michael Jackson

lannoo

CONTENTS

- 11 No small beer
- 15 Beer sommelier Ben Vinken
- 19 The various styles of beer
- 29 How is beer made?
- 45 The ritual of the beer sommelier
- 51 The rules of pairing beer and food

- 55 Abbaye des Rocs
- 56 Achel Blond
- 61 Adriaen Brouwer
- 62 Affligem Blond
- 65 Augustijn
- 66 Boon Oude Kriek
- 69 Bornem Tripel
- 70 Brigand
- 73 Brugge Tripel
- 74 Brugse Straffe Hendrik
- 76 Brugse Zot
- 79 Bush Grand Prestige
- 80 Chimay Cinq Cents
- 83 Chimay Grande Réserve
- 84 Corsendonk Agnus & Pater
- 87 De Koninck
- 88 Delirium Tremens
- 90 Deus Brut des Flandres
- 93 Double Enghien
- 94 Drie Fonteinen Oude Geuze
- 96 Duchesse de Bourgogne
- 98 Duvel
- 101 Ename Tripel
- 102 Gouden Carolus Classic
- 107 Grimbergen Blond
- 109 Grottenbier
- 110 Gulden Draak
- 112 Hapkin
- 115 Hoegaarden
- 116 Kasteel Bruin & Tripel
- 119 Keizer Karel Bruin
- 120 La Chouffe
- 122 Leffe Blond

- 125 Liefmans Gouden Band
- 126 Liefmans Kriek
- 129 Lindemans Cuvée René and Kriek
- 131 Malheur Brut Réserve
- 135 Malheur 10
- 136 Maredsous 6 & 8
- 138 Mort Subite Oude Kriek
- 140 Orval
- 143 Palm Spéciale
- 144 Palm Royale
- 147 Pater Lieven Blond
- 148 Pauwel Kwak
- 150 Petrus Gouden Tripel
- 153 Poperings Hommelbier
- 154 Rochefort 8
- 157 Rodenbach
- 160 Saison Dupont
- 165 Satan Red
- 166 Serafijn Celtic Angel
- 168 St Bernardus Abt
- 170 St Feuillien Triple
- 173 Timmermans Caveau Oude Geuze
- 174 Tongerlo Tripel Blond
- 176 Tripel Karmeliet
- 179 Westmalle Tripel
- 183 Wittekerke Rosé

- 187 Index

NO SMALL BEER

Beer is a popular drink all over the world. But while in practically all countries it is mainly pils that is drunk, and the supply is mostly confined to a few brands, things are rather different in Belgium. The Belgians enjoy about three-quarters of their total consumption of beer in the shape of refreshing, bottom-fermented beers, but one quarter consists of an unbelievably wide range of special beers brewed using three different fermentation methods: top, spontaneous and mixed fermentation.

We will explain these concepts in detail later in this book. Clearly it was well worth the trouble to devote one issue in the ¡*Foodie!* range to beer, and for this I have selected sixty-four exceptional beers from the more than four hundred which Belgium boasts: I will give a short account of each beer, with a description of my tasting results and a suggested dish to go with it. Moreover, I poured a glass of each beer for our photographer Joris Luyten, who has made such eye-catching photographs of them that your mouth waters just looking at them.

This book comes out just the right moment: today's beer lovers are more sophisticated than previous generations. After a hard day's work they no longer feel like tossing off any old six-pack of pils, but choose a geuze or a white beer as an aperitif. Then with their evening meal they drink a nice abbey beer or regional beer, whether or not poured from a large bottle. An elegant sampling glass is then sometimes more appropriate than the large classic goblet or cup-shaped glasses so typical of our Belgian beer culture.

No small beer

Only when we Belgians go abroad do we fully realize the towering image of our beers: 'Are you from Belgium? Oh, we like your beer and your chocolates!' That is also reflected in the figures: more than 55 per cent of our beer production is exported. Everywhere in the world our beer styles are copied, particularly in countries where a culture of small breweries has developed (the US, Canada, Denmark, France, Italy…). But there is also an enormous respect for our art of brewing: 'Belgium' always stands for quality, eccentricity, individuality and creativity. We have so many aromas, colours and flavours that it is well nigh impossible to arrange them all into categories or beer styles. Nor is my attempt – in the form of this book – the last word, but I describe the kinds of beer as broadly as possible, so that everyone can recognize them.

I hope reading this book on beer, in which I have tried to put across my experience of nearly thirty years of beer tasting, will give you great pleasure.

Cheers!
Ben Vinken

BEN VINKEN, BEER SOMMELIER

Beer is the main thread running through Ben Vinken's varied career. In 1979 he started work as a lawyer in the Lamot Brewery, and later carried out sales and marketing functions successively with Palm Brewery and Interbrew (now Inbev).

Since 1992 he has worked as a journalist and publisher of publications specializing in beer, such as Michael Jacksons's *'Great Beers of Belgium'* and *Bierpassie Magazine*. He is also a specialist in the field of 'beer brand development', and has developed numerous marketing campaigns for various breweries.

In addition Ben Vinken writes columns in the *Gazet van Antwerpen* and *Het Belang van Limburg*, and contributes an article on beer in the monthly *Ambiance*. He also wrote and co-produced the TV series Bierpassie for ATV and recently started a new series with Vitaya, *De Bier Sommelier*. Finally every year in June he organizes the *'Beer Passion Weekend'* in his home town Antwerp.

Ben learnt his trade with the great Michael Jackson, the British beer author who died in 2007 and was the first to describe beers as if they were wines – in a splendid jargon – and discover the gastronomic qualities of Belgian beers, making the whole world aware of them.

Like a true sommelier Ben guides you in this ¡Foodie Beer! through the jungle of beer styles in which Belgium is so rich, and gives detailed information about some sixty special brews which he selected and tasted.

We are convinced that together with beer sommelier Ben Vinken everyone will be able to make the right choice of beer for every occasion.

The chapter 'How is beer made?' was written by master brewer Jef Van den Steen, the author of various books on beer and a journalist for *Bierpassie (Beer Passion) Magazine*.

THE VARIOUS STYLES OF BEER

Bottom Fermentation
This fermentation happens with pure cultures of 'bottom-fermenting yeasts' (saccharomyces carlsbergensis) at a low temperature (5-10°C) followed by a cold 'maturing' at around 0°C, for a longer or shorter period.

The first pils beer was Pilsner Urquell from the Czech town of Pilsen, which gave its name to this style of beer. The beer is characterized by its golden colour, white head, low alcohol content and dry, bitter finish. Pils dominates the world of beer and accounts for 95 per cent of world production. In this book, however, we devote no more attention to it.

Top fermentation
This fermentation happens with pure cultures of 'top-fermenting yeasts' (saccharomyces cerevisiae) at 15-25°C and, depending on the choice of yeast, leads to fruitiness or a phenolic smoky aroma. A second fermentation in the bottle produces extra pith and complexity.

Most of the beers in this book are top fermentation. We can categorize these further as follows:

Abbey beers

Abbey beers are brewed by lay brewers under licence from an abbey, or called after a saint.

Affligem Blond

Augustijn

Bornem Tripel

Corsendonk Agnus

Corsendonk Pater

Ename Tripel

Grimbergen Blond

Grimbergen Cuvée de l'Ermitage

Leffe Blond

Maredsous 8

Maredsous 10

Pater Lieven Blond

Petrus Gouden Tripel

Tongerlo Tripel blond

Tripel Karmeliet

St. Feuillien Triple

Trappists

These are beers brewed *intra muros* at a trappist (Cistercian) monastery.

Achel Blond

Achel Extra Bruin

Chimay Cinq Cents

Chimay Grande Réserve

Orval
Westmalle Dubbel
Westmalle Tripel

Regional beers

These are, as the name suggests, regional beers brewed in a specific estate, town or region.

Abbaye des Rocs
Adriaen Brouwer
Brugge Tripel
Brugse Zot
Bush Grand Prestige
Double Enghien
Gouden Carolus Classic
Gouden Carolus Triple
Grottenbier
Gulden Draak
Kasteel Bruin
Kasteel Tripel
Keizer Karel Bruin
La Chouffe
Malheur 10
Pauwel Kwak
Poperings Hommelbier
Satan Red
Serafijn Celtic Angel
Straffe Hendrik

White beers
White (wheat) beers are sweet yet sharp beers based on malt and wheat with coriander.

Hoegaarden
Wittekerke Rosé

Spéciale Belge
These are amber-coloured beers, easily drinkable and malty.

De Koninck
Palm Spéciale
Palm Royale

Saisons
A refreshing style of Walloon beer, hoppy and thirst-quenching.

Avec les bons voeux
Saison Dupont
Moinette Blonde

Strong blond beers
Pale, strong beers with devilish names.

Delirium Tremens
Duvel
Hapkin

The various styles of beer

Bière Brut

This is a new style of beer. The basis is a strong, blond beer that is matured by the *méthode champenoise*, with *rémuage* and *dégorgement*.

Deus Brut des Flandres
Malheur Brut Réserve

Mixed fermentation

The main fermentation at 15 to 25°C happens with a 'mixed culture' of high yeasts and lactic acid flora. Maturation on oak for two years turns the organic acids into a complex fruitiness, as it does in wine. The tannins of the oak give a mouth-filling, drying, oaky taste.

Duchesse de Bourgogne
Liefmans Gouden Band
Liefmans Kriek
Rodenbach
Rodenbach Grand Cru

Spontaneous fermentation

In wild fermentation the brew cools in the open cooling vat where it is spontaneously fertilized with wild yeasts (brettanomyces bruxellencis and lambicus) from the air around. Fermentation and lengthy maturation in the vats turns the brew into a fruity, slightly sour lambic. Geuze is a mixture of young and old lambics, fermented in the bottle. Old Lambic, Old Geuze and Old Kriek are beer styles protected in the EU. Maceration of cherries or raspberries on 100 per cent lambic gives an authentic quality fruit beer.

Boon Oude Kriek
Drie Fonteinen Oude Geuze
Lindemans Cuvée René
Mort Subite Oude Kriek
Timmermans Geuze Caveau

HOW IS BEER MADE?

Brewing: past and present

Brewing beer is a skill that is centuries old – it is thought to have started in Mesopotamia between 10,000 and 4,000 BC and in the course of time evolved from a rather mysterious and mystical occupation (no-one understood how fermentation started and precisely what happened) to a trade lacking any sense of romance. It's not for nothing that these days engineers specialized in brewing keep a tight hold on proceedings in the brewery.

The basic products have actually hardly changed: water; grain as a source of starch; herbs and spices to add taste; and of course, yeast to turn the sugars present in the mix into alcohol and carbon dioxide.

The raw materials

As far as quantity is concerned, **water** is the most important ingredient: beer consists 85 to 95 per cent of water, and in the production process five to eight litres of water are needed for each litre of beer. The most important requirement the brewer lays down for the water he uses is that it is clean and bacteriologically pure. In a thickly populated and heavily industrial country like Belgium, surface water is, of course, out of the question. Spring water is ideal, but also well water from deep layers (100 metres deep or more) and tap water come into consideration.

The grain used most for brewing is **barley**, although in Belgium a great deal of **wheat** is used too, particularly in brewing white beer and lambic, the basic beer for Oude Geuze, Faro, Oude Kriek, and similar. These grains contain starch which first has to be turned into fermentable sugar. Particularly barley by nature possesses many enzymes which can start up this conversion process. These enzymes are activated during the malting. This is in fact an imitation of what happens in nature: letting the grain sprout. But before any new plants can grow out of the grain the germination process is halted in the oast house, by drying in the kiln. Depending on the temperature at which the sprouting grain is kilned, the maltster gets *pale malt* or *pils malt* (which keeps the natural colour of the grain), *caramel malt* (in which the sugars are caramelized, giving an amber colour to the beer), or *toasted malt* (which is, of course, black).

As well as malt (of barley or wheat), unmalted grains are also used in brewing to replace part of the malt, which is more expensive. These malt substitutes are called **adjuncts**. The most commonly used adjunct in Belgium is maize, particularly in the production of pils.

In special beers **sugar** is most likely to be used. It increases the density and so also the alcohol content of the beer, without adding other, less digestible elements. But sugars also play an important role in influencing the colour (for example, by darker candy), and for a second fermentation in the bottle.

The typical bitter taste and smell of beer is achieved by adding **hops** during boiling; an additional advantage of this is that the action of the hops is bacteriostatic, in other words, it curbs the growth of bacteria so that the beer keeps longer. As well as hops, Belgian brewers also use a variety of herbs and spices to give their beer a particular flavour. So almost all white beers contain coriander and curaçao (=dried orange peel), while star anise, lady's bedstraw, liquorice, paradise grains, etcetera, give a unique taste to some special beers.

Finally: no beer without **yeast**! It is, after all, the yeast that converts the sugars (from the malt, the adjuncts and the added sugars) into alcohol and carbon dioxide. *Wild yeasts and cultured yeasts* are distinguished according to the form in which they are produced. Wild yeasts occur freely in nature, cultured yeasts are grown in brewers' laboratories. Belgium is the only country in the world where beer is fermented using four different methods of fermentation.

The oldest method is spontaneous fermentation in which the brewer adds no yeast. The fermentation comes about spontaneously, as it were, from the wild yeasts present in the surrounding atmosphere. This centuries-old way of fermenting is still used in the brewing of lambic in Payottenland (a farming area west of Brussels). A more recent method, but no less complex, is the mixed fermentation, in which as well as wild yeasts, cultured yeasts are also active. Particularly in East and West Flanders this method is still used in the production of old brown, such as Liefmans and Rodenbach.

The two methods used most are bottom and top fermentation. Pils is a typical bottom-fermented beer: the yeast works best at a low temperature of about 6 to 10°C: after fermenting for about ten

days the yeast sinks to the bottom of the vat. Belgian special beers, such as, for instance, trappist and abbey beer, *spéciale Belge*, white beers and *saisons*, are top fermented. Top fermentation yeast works best between 15 and 25°C and the fermentation does not last so long (4 to 6 days). The fermentation is much more intense than in the bottom fermentation, and the yeast forms a thick layer above the young beer.

Of course, sometimes yet other raw materials are used, such as fruit for the fruit beers, or rice in some pils beers. But it would take us too long to discuss all of them.

Brewing

Before you can start brewing, the necessary quantity of malt must be weighed out and – to make the grain content more soluble – the malt must be milled. The quantity of malt per litre of water determines the eventual alcohol content, and the kind of malt selected (pale, caramel or toasted) determines the colour.

The actual brewing begins with making the **mash**, the mixture of milled malt with the heated brewing water. This mash is then heated, either by means of a naked flame (heat directly under the kettle) or by steam spirals (indirect heating). At some critical temperatures – those at which specific enzymes work best – a rest period is imposed. Temperatures around 62 and 72°C are particularly important; that is when the **conversion to sugar** of the malt starch takes place. Finally the mash is heated still further to 78°C or more to put a stop to the activity of the enzymes.

Then follows the **filtration**: this has the object of separating the liquid malt extract (*wort*) from the solid parts (*draff*). The draff is sold to farmers as a valuable cattle food, the wort is a sugary liquid which for various reasons must be boiled. During the **boiling** the water evaporates, so that the density, that is to say the quantity of fermentable sugar per litre, is reduced to the desired level.

This boiling should continue for at least an hour, the time that is needed for the alpha acids of the hop to isomerize. Or to put it more simply: to cause the bitter substances of the hops to dissolve. Finally there is the **sterilization effect**: during boiling there is a breakdown of the proteins in which coagulating proteins flake out and can then be easily removed.

After boiling the *hoppy* wort has to be cooled as fast as possible to the fermentation temperature. But for this, the remains of the hops and the broken down proteins have to be removed. **Cooling** is done by means of a heat-exchanger. Cold water is pumped in through a closed system of pipes, in counter flow with the boiling wort, so that the cold water is heated and the boiling wort cooled. That hot water can then be used to clean up afterwards or to start up another brew.

The fermentation

After cooling the wort goes to the fermenting tanks and the yeast is introduced. As long as there is acid present in the wort, the yeast will go on multiplying. When all the acid has been absorbed, the yeast starts to convert the sugar into roughly equal parts of *alcohol* and *carbon dioxide*. During the main fermentation the major part of the sugar is fermented. Then the beer, for that is what it now is, starts to **lager** – to mature. During this stage, which mostly goes on at a relatively low temperature (even down to a minus degree), the sugars still remaining ferment and the beer can take up a quantity of carbon dioxide. Then the yeast and the other solid residues sink to the bottom of the tank, so that the beer becomes clear.

These solid residues are later removed during filtration and the clear beer is pumped into a tank for *clarified beer*, where it is usually mixed with other brews to achieve an end product that is as consistent as possible.

Conditioning

The beer is now ready to be filled into barrels, bottles or cans. Because the consumer expects a bubbling and foaming beer, the brewer must make sure that it contains enough carbon dioxide. This can be done in two ways, by saturation or a second fermentation.

With a few exceptions beer in barrels is always saturated and this is always the case with cans. *Saturation* is saturating the beer with carbon dioxide under pressure. The colder the beer, the faster the operation proceeds. Saturated beers are immediately ready for drinking, although they are often also pasteurized to prevent the development of bacteria and any possible second fermentation. Pasteurization consists of a brief heating of the beer to above 60°C; bacteria harmful to the beer are killed at this temperature. Many bottled beers, too, and particularly those intended for 'easy drinking', are saturated and pasteurized in this way.

A second fermentation in bottles or in barrels (never in cans) may require less expensive machinery, but demands more knowledge and experience, and is never used with bottom fermentation. For a second fermentation a carefully worked out quantity of *sugar* and *young, active yeast* is added to the beer. Then the bottles or barrels go to the 'warm room', where the temperature is always kept above 20°C. Just as in the main fermentation process, the yeast turns the sugar into alcohol, so that the alcohol content rises slightly, and into carbon dioxide, so that the beer becomes naturally saturated. After two, or at most three weeks (for top fermentation beers), all the added sugars have fermented and the yeast sediment sinks to the bottom. In spontaneously fermented beers, such as Old Geuze, this stage lasts six months and both more sugar and more yeast is added. Second fermentation beers are easily recognizable by the yeast residues in the bottle. They will consequently have to be handled carefully when pouring them out, or the yeast sediment will shake loose and the beer goes cloudy. There is actually nothing wrong with it – clarity is in itself not a sign of quality. Moreover, beer yeast is a source of vitamin B and therefore very healthy – it is even sold in health food shops in the form of tablets. But many beer lovers still prefer their beer clear.

After the second fermentation the beer is ready to drink, but the beer lover, or beer expert, would rather leave it to mature for a few more weeks, preferably at cellar temperature (8-12°C), and – more importantly – at as constant a temperature as possible, and with minimum exposure to light. That is in fact why beer bottles are always made of coloured glass (green or brown).

In contrast to pasteurized beers, which keep a constant taste and aroma for several months, the taste of second fermentation beers evolves – they are, after all, live beers. This also applies to beers that have a second fermentation in the barrel, but barrel beer is drunk more quickly and is therefore usually a little more fruity.

Jef Van den Steen

THE BEER SOMMELIER'S RITUAL

Pouring

If you serve beer in the same way as you serve wine or champagne, you will soon regard it quite differently. All at once drinking a beverage usually considered 'commonplace' becomes a celebratory experience, thanks to just a few simple actions.

First the bottle: if you chill a three-quarter litre bottle in an ice bucket, and you use elegant tasting glasses with long stems like the ones used for champagne, you create a very sophisticated perception of your beer. Most of today's leading Belgian beers are available in handsome 75 cl bottles. For this we have to thank export markets, where this size is much in demand. In Belgium a chain of shops has recently been established specializing in this size: the O'Cool/Covée beer corner quoting some sixty brands in such bottles is very impressive.

When the ice bucket with the colourful bottle (beer labels are always more flashy than wine labels) is put on the table, the party can start. You carefully loosen the wire muzzle over the cork, Then you grip the cork firmly between your thumb and your index finger and you give a careful twist at the bottom of the bottle in the opposite direction; in this way you apply more strength, while you keep the whole thing under control with your other hand. Do it all slowly and carefully, because beer froths and too brusque a movement can easily lead to an explosive moment. With a little 'plop' you take the cork out of the bottle, which always releases a little vapour. Then lay the cork and muzzle beside the ice bucket and hold the bottle at an angle to pour. With champagne bottles (in Belgium beer is always in a champagne bottle with a recessed bottom or in a so-called 'Belgian' bottle, which is straighter and without a recess) you can put your thumb underneath in the recess (the 'soul' of the bottle) and pour it like a real sommelier. Pour it in gently, without gushing, so that you keep the froth under control and don't shake the yeast loose from the bottom of the bottle. A 20 cl taster glass is quickly filled, but that is ideal, because the ice bucket remains on the table, so that the beer stays cool to go on being poured.

A question often asked is: 'Is it a good thing to serve beer so cold?' My answer to that is quite simple: by serving beer cold, you leave the choice open for everyone. If you like it cold, you can start drinking straightaway. If you prefer it a little warmer, then let it wait a bit, or warm it in your hands. But a beer that is served warm will not get cold again!

Tasting

At last we have reached the stage where we can begin to sample our beer. And for this you need all your senses. To start with your eyes: you can admire the beer because of the colour, its sparkle and its head of foam. There are many shades of colour in beer, dependant on the malt used. In our Belgian beers all ranges of colour are opened up, and that, too, is reflected in this book. From pale, amber, blond, gold, white, rosé, red and brown to a chocolate colour and all shades between these basic colours, you will find them all in our treasury of national beers. Rising bubbles of carbon dioxide with fluctuating energy, dependent on the saturation of the beer. Some brewers even make a scratch in their glass to make it all bubble more (isn't that true, Duvel?). And then the head: it can be thin, thick, fine, sticking to the side, or weak, and it takes its colour from the malt. For example, in Westmalle Dubbel you have an attractive light brown head reminiscent of *caffelatte*, a true Kriek has a pale pink head, a white beer a true white one. Wonderful, isn't it?

The second sense brought into play (we have not really started tasting yet), is the nose. My good friend Jef Van den Steen always claims that you can taste beer for 70 per cent with your nose. I don't disagree with him. Many brewers' secrets are given away in the aroma. Before you begin to smell (what is called nosing by whiskey tasters) swirl your glass round well, so that the aromas can be freely released. Then sniff the aroma right into your nose. You can smell malt, hop, herbs and spices, fruit… and you can also smell at once whether the beer is still fresh or musty. You have to drink beer when it is young, it is – with a few exceptions – made to be drunk fresh, it should certainly be no more than one year old. If a beer is oxidized (because, for instance, it has stood too long in the cellar, or was badly drawn off) you will smell the defect immediately. And just as with wine, you send a bad bottle straight back to your supplier. Fortunately that does not happen so often with beer.

And then the actual tasting. You take a good mouthful and let the beer roll over your tongue for a moment. On the front of the tongue you taste sweetness, next to it saltiness (which does not occur in beer), in the middle of the tongue herbal tastes, and on the edges acidity. You experience bitterness only at the back of the tongue and particularly when you swallow. So we never spit the beer out, in contrast to our rather barbaric wine friends. When you swallow, also sniff (breath through your nose); in this way you bring the aromas warmed up along your throat to the back of your nose, and that gives an additional olfactory tasting sensation, particularly for classifying delicate aromatic components.

Look, smell, taste – and then we have only dealt with the beer itself. If we are going to eat anything with it, only then will our tasting experience be complete!

THE RULE FOR PAIRING BEER AND FOOD

The combination of beer and gastronomy was until recently still mainly associated with the addition of beer to a sauce. You can 'deglaze' a sauce with a spoonful of beer and then you will taste a pleasant bitterness in the sauce, at least if you have not left it to boil too long, because then it might well become a bit *too* bitter. But there are so many possibilities for beer in the kitchen. The first chef who wanted to make this plain to me was Jan Buytaert of the starred restaurant De Bellefleur in Kapellen. Jan thought that you would be doing a brewer an injustice if you only used his beer in sauces: 'He has put so much of his soul into it!' So Jan combines all sorts of dishes with beer. And beer can accentuate (and complement) the taste of a dish or it can contrast with it. Another great pioneer in the field of pairing beer and food is the New Yorker Garrett Oliver, the master brewer of the Brooklyn Brewery. A few years ago he wrote his best-selling *The Brewmaster's Table* in which he matched hundreds of beers from all over the world with dishes. Since a true beer revolution was going on in America at the time, with thousands of micro breweries, and consequently the 'taste' conquered the country again, the moment was ripe to pair these beers with an up to date cuisine. The complex tastes of special beers could magically convert an everyday dish into a festive one. It has become an affordable luxury. Whether you combine a fruity white beer with a goat cheese salad, or a spicy dish with a mild *spéciale Belge*, or a rich Trappist with a substantial steak, or a fruity *framboise* with a slice of chocolate gateau, for each meal you can always find the perfect beer to partner it. And in the right combinations it is not only the dish, but also the beer that tastes the better for it.

This is why in this book we will suggest a suitable dish for each beer.

ABBAYE DES ROCS   REGIONAL BEER

Brewer Jean-Marie Eloir from the Hainault village of Montignies-sur-Rocs (near Mons) first began brewing in his garage. During the day he worked in a mortgage registry office, copying documents. He found brewing more entertaining and gradually managed to earn enough from brewing to make a profession out of a hobby. Although less widely known in Flanders, his *Abbaye des Rocs*, brewed with six different kinds of malt and four different spices (curaçao, ginger, paradise grains, and liquorice) is in fact a very special beer. The label on the bottle refers to an abbey (a non-existent one), but the brewer gets the yeast with which the beer is made from Rochefort and Westmalle bottles.

The *Abbaye des Rocs* beers are sold worldwide and have won several prizes. With his daughter Nathalie (a brewing engineer) the future of the brewery is assured.

Abbaye des Rocs 9% vol. alc.

BREWED BY Brasserie de l'Abbaye des Rocs, Montignies-sur-Roc

STYLE dark regional beer

BEN'S TASTING NOTES substantial, complex, spicy beer with the sweetness of the alcohol; strong and bitter hop finish; classed among the *grands crus* of the Walloon country

FOOD PAIRING an enjoyable picnic in front of an open fire, or with a well-seasoned dish of game

ACHEL BLOND TRAPPIST

In the first issue of *Beer Passion Magazine*, in December 1998, there is a report on the opening of a trappist micro-brewery. The Cistercians of Achel were looking for ways to maintain their abbey. Until then they had been active in agriculture, but the work became too strong for them and did not attract any young monks. They consulted their brothers of Westmalle, who sent their good old brother Thomas to Achel. He was the man who had perfected Westmalle Triple and so created a world classic from hops, malt and yeast. Could he now do the same for Achel? Brother Thomas, who had by then retired to a Liège retreat, travelled to Achel, where he made a blond beer and a 6 per cent brown beer which was at first only available from the barrel in the reception suite next to the micro-brewery. Later the beers were bottled, more specifically the 8 per cent blond version refermented in bottle, and the 8 per cent brown, as well as a 9.5 per cent extra brown. The beers were bottled in a friendly neighbouring brewery, as there was no filling line in Achel. After Brother Thomas's health deteriorated, Brother Antoine from

Achel Blond 8% vol. alc.

BREWED BY St Benedict's Abbey, Achel

BEN'S TASTING NOTES very fruity and dry (Saaz hops) with some touches of citrus, substantial with a very dry finish; a perfect aperitif

FOOD PAIRING try this some time with tuna grilled on a barbecue, with a sweet soya sauce; the beer contrasts with it perfectly

Rochefort lent a hand, and now it is Brother Jules who holds the mashing fork, helped by a lay brewer, Marc Knops. All the Achel beers have a generous aroma of hops and the astringency on which brother Thomas was so keen. Around the abbey there are splendid walking and cycling tracks and in summer it is a pleasant place to visit, in the knowledge that a fresh and hoppy Achel awaits you on the inviting terrace of the brewery.

Cheers!

Achel Extra Bruin 9,5% vol. alc.

BREWED BY St Benedict's Abbey, Achel

BEN'S TASTING NOTES a substantial brew, made with dark candy sugar and a fruity touch of herbs

FOOD PAIRING ideal with a chocolate dessert or a good Havana cigar

ADRIAEN BROUWER REGIONAL BEER

In 2007 the brothers Lode and Carlo Roman were presented with the *Meesters van de Gerst* (Barley Masters) prize by Michael Jackson. Their centuries-old brewery (see also Ename Triple under Abbey Beers) is known particularly for its Oudenarde brown, the popular 5 per cent brown beer that is drunk in gallons in the local cafés instead of (or as well as) pils. A few years ago the brothers rechristened this beer Adriaen Brouwer, after the famous sixteenth-century painter who was born in Oudenarde and who is now remembered every year during the Adriaen Brouwer festival.

A fervent devotee of this brown beer lives in the neighbouring district of Brakel; Herman De Croo, former president of the Belgian parliament, sometimes binges at 20 parties a day and swears by the Oudenarde Brown, soft, nice, and very easy to drink.

Adriaen Brouwer 5% vol. alc.

BREWED BY Brouwerij Roman, Mater, Oudenarde

STYLE brown regional beer

BEN'S TASTING NOTES lively aroma of oranges that develops against a background of soft, sweetish malt, with hints of chocolate and toast

FOOD PAIRING just let a Flemish carbonade stew gently (and drink the beer with it and after it)

Adriaen Brouwer

AFFLIGEM BLOND   ABBEY BEER

Since the 1970s the Benedictine abbey of Affligem has had its abbey beers brewed under licence by the De Smedt brewery in Opwijk, which for some years has simply been called the Affligem Brewery, after its most famous beer. Affligem has by now become a leading brand, with production this year exceeding 200,000 hectolitres, thanks particularly to their cooperation with Heineken, which has for years distributed this beer in the Netherlands and France and recently took over the brewery completely. In the Netherlands it is mainly the double (the brown) which runs from the taps; in France the blond. There is also a triple, which in 2004 and 2008 won the World Beer Cup in the triples class, and the hoppy Christmas beer *Patersvat*, made with their own hops from Affligem. The *Affligem Blond* is the brewery's 'bestseller' – both from the barrel and bottled – a delightful, informal, fresh and fruity blond abbey beer, which still tastes like more.

Affligem Blond 7% vol. alc.

BREWED BY	Brouwerij Affligem BDS, Opwijk
STYLE	blond abbey beer
BEN'S TASTING NOTES	fruity aroma with a sweetish accent; a light fruit taste with a pleasant, bitter finish
FOOD PAIRING	fresh salads, grilled salmon

AUGUSTIJN ABBEY BEER

This is an odd-one-out among abbey beers. First of all in colour: it is more amber coloured, which is unusual in an abbey beer. On the label is a brewer priest, there is no mention of an abbey. The beer is brewed by the Van Steenberge family's rather unusual Bios brewery in Ertvelde, which leads a discreet existence and does not go in for marketing. *Augustijn* is pretty much their best known brand, and has links with the Augustinian abbey in Ghent, to which it still pays some dues. The beer has a second fermentation in the bottle, which gives it a very special taste. This is also the case with its slightly heavier brother, *Augustijn Grand Cru*. Both beers have been given a special culture of yeast for the second fermentation, in which brettanomyces are also present. These wild yeasts produce a slightly acidic taste.

Augustijn 8% vol. alc.

BREWED BY Brouwerij Van Steenberge (Bios), Ertvelde

STYLE dark abbey beer (although the colour is in fact more like amber)

BEN'S TASTING NOTES malty with spicy accents in the nose; full balanced taste with a creamy feel in the mouth and a bitter finish

FOOD PAIRING paté de campagne

BOON OUDE KRIEK <small>SPONTANEOUS FERMENTATION</small>

Frank Boon is a 'geuze revivalist'. He has done his enormous best to keep alive and promote the tiny beer segment of Old Geuze, a category protected by Europe and the only *appellation controlé* in Belgium, mostly by making fantastic products himself. Boon's old geuze beers from Lembeek in Brabant (from which the name Lambic comes) are mainly known for their mellow geuzes. As well as the Old Geuze there is also *Marriage Parfait*, a geuze with an admixture of mainly five-year-old lambic.

His best-selling beer is *Boon Kriek*, but the gem of his brewery is his *Boon Oude Kriek*. This is made by the addition of 400 grams (per litre) of small, wild cherries (*krieken*) to eighteen-months-old lambic. After a fermenting maceration the beer undergoes a second fermentation in the bottle.

Boon Oude Kriek 6,5% vol. alc.

BREWED BY Lambiekbrouwerij Boon, Lembeek

STYLE old kriek (cherry beer)

BEN'S TASTING NOTES rosé coloured liquid and head, aromas of wood, tannin, hints of animal, complemented by a light impression of cherries; long, slightly bitter finish

BORNEM TRIPEL <small>ABBEY BEER</small>

The Bios brewery (see p. 65) also has another range of abbey beers on its list, one linked now for at least fifty years with the abbey of Bornem. In the 1950s the brewers discovered all the commercial possibilities of abbey beer. For instance, Leffe started in 1952 (when your humble servant was born!), Tongerlo in 1954, and Affligem in 1956. In 1957 Pater Lieven, Postel and Bornem were put on the market, to be followed barely a year later by Grimbergen and Steenbrugge.

The abbey of St Bernard in Bornem gave its name to a beer brewed by the Beirens brewery in Wommelgem. It was inspired by Hendrik Verlinden, a member of the Beirens family, and a brewing father of all their triples (he made the Westmalle Tripel in 1933). In 1971 the brand came into the hands of the Steenberge family, who immediately used it for second fermentation beers. *Bornem Tripel* is my favourite beer in their range.

Bornem Tripel 9% vol. alc.

BREWED BY Brouwerij Van Steenberge (Bios), Ertvelde

STYLE triple abbey beer

BEN'S TASTING NOTES aromas of liquorice, hop and coriander; fairly sweet initial taste, progressing into a slightly bitter finish

FOOD PAIRING bouillabaisse

BRIGAND   STRONG BLOND BEER

I will make no secret of it: *Brigand* is one of my favourite beers. That is, of course, a very personal view, and they know that at the brewery. When I get there, the first thing they ask is: 'A Brigand, Ben?' Of course it is all to do with the taste, which is quite unique. And nothing has been changed, only the colour has become a little blonder. And the packaging has been thoroughly revamped. But amber or blond, *Brigand* has always been ranged among the

strong blond beers (the 'devilish' or 'wicked beers'), although in the past it was more of an amber colour. Meanwhile brewmaster Jozef Maes has adjusted that defect. *Brigand* now looks a nice blond, and this is emphasized by the decorative, elegant and exclusive, tall goblet. This glass, combined with the 75 cl bottle, produces a champagne-like impression, and so we go back to the time when the beer was launched, in the early 1980s, when Van Honsebrouck senior made a hit with Club Brugge, St Louis and *Brigand*, which was served in large bottles with corks and blue tinfoil.

Xavier Van Honsebrouck is still looking for a good slogan. A *Brigand*: isn't that a Jean-Marie De Decker character, the Belgian judo coach turned politician and a born obstructionist? And if you drink a Brigand, don't you look as if you are a real macho man who doesn't necessarily agree with everything. Xavier hasn't got there yet, but he can see that this is the direction where he will end up. So a beer for people who dare go against the stream. And who like a strong beer, with a slightly sour taste.

Brigand 9% vol. alc.

BREWED BY Brouwerij van Honsebrouck, Ingelmunster

STYLE strong blond regional beer

BEN'S TASTING NOTES strong, spicy and slightly bitter beer, with a full taste and touches of malt, coriander, cloves and orange

FOOD PAIRING good with monk fish

BRUGGE TRIPEL   REGIONAL BEER

Currently there is only one town brewery in Bruges: the 'Halve Maan' (Half Moon) on the Walplein. Until a few years ago the 'Gouden Boom' (Golden Tree) of Palm Breweries in the Langestraat was also operating, but this site eventually closed. Not for long, in fact, since new brewing activities are planned for it, although they will be rather limited and have a tourist bias. *Brugge Tripel* beer comes from the Gouden Boom, a beer that we clearly don't class among abbey beers, but as a town beer. Currently it is brewed in Steenhuffel. In its tall flute glass the blond beer leaves a tracing of good Bruges lace, the aroma is floral and hoppy, and the taste bitter, rich and creamy. Sometimes you can also find this beer in barrel and then it tastes even softer and fruitier.

Brugge Tripel 8,7% vol. alc.

BREWED BY Palm Breweries, Steenhuffel

STYLE triple town beer

BEN'S TASTING NOTES good golden blond; firm head; hop in the aroma; bitter, rich taste with a mostly malty character; long, warming and dry finish

FOOD PAIRING excellent with well-seasoned preparations of rabbit, partridge or quail; also good with monk fish or lobster

BRUGSE STRAFFE HENDRIK REGIONAL BEER

Straffe Hendrik was originally a Bruges beer brewed in the Halve Maan (Half Moon) brewery in Bruges. In type it is really a Flemish saison and in this category it actually carried off the gold medal of the World Beer Cup in Seattle in 2006.

In 1989 the Riva Brewery took over the Halve Maan house brewery on the Walplein in Bruges, renovated the site into a tourist attraction and brewed just *Straffe Hendrik* there. This beer is now brewed in Dentergem by Liefmans Breweries, while the buildings of the Halve Maan are again being exploited by the owners, the Maes family. The famous Bruges beer is still brewed according to an ancient recipe, and rightly takes its place among the Flemish *saisons*.

Brugse Straffe Hendrik 6% vol. alc.

BREWED BY	Liefmans Breweries, Dentergem
STYLE	blond regional beer, Flemish *saison*
BEN'S TASTING NOTES	a hint of fruit, hops and even metal in the aroma; more lightly sweet than bitter in taste, and easily drinkable
FOOD PAIRING	serve with a light, savoury, fish dish

BRUGSE ZOT   REGIONAL BEER

As soon as Palm closed the doors of the Gouden Boom (Golden Tree), fresh brewing activity started up in Bruges, and once more in the old buildings of the former Halve Maan brewery of the Maes family. This brewery had actually only been inactive for three years, and the last beer that was brewed in it was the Bruges Straffe Hendrik, under contract for Liefmans breweries. With the disappearance of the Gouden Boom, Xavier Vanneste, Veronique Maes's son, saw a golden opportunity. He would light the fires under the brew kettles again and sell the beer in the successful brasserie on the site on the Walplein in Bruges, which had meanwhile become available (Riva/Liefmans had forgotten to renew their lease agreement). His plan was a bold one, but he was successful all along the line; *Brugse Zot* and soon also *Brugse Zot Dubbel* won almost all the prizes available internationally and the brasserie is visited by more than a hundred thousand people a year. Exports are good, too. The name *Brugse Zot* (Bruges Fool) refers to an anecdote about the emperor of Austria. When he was asked to found an asylum in Bruges he answered that if they would just shut the town gates, the whole of Bruges could serve as an asylum.

Brugse Zot 6% vol. alc.

BREWED BY Brouwerij de Halve Maan, Brugge

STYLE blond town beer

BEN'S TASTING NOTES aromas of yeast and citrus fruit, which also come through in the taste; a dry and refreshing beer

FOOD PAIRING pithy salads, scampi with curry sauce

BUSH GRAND PRESTIGE   REGIONAL BEER

Bush is just about the heaviest beer in Belgium. I drank it for the first time during a visit to Tournai in 1986, 'the year of the beer'. It was brewed by the Dubuisson family in Pipaix, on the road from Tournai to Mons. In 2008 this beer has already been around for 75 years! *Buisson* is the French word for a bush or shrub. Hence the name – which then created problems in America (because of the Anheuser Busch Company of, among others, Budweiser beer), so that the beer is called Scaldis there, the Latin name of the Scheldt, which flows near Pipaix.

This sweet, amber-coloured and very strong beer gets yet another dimension when it has lain for some months on young American oak. These barrels were installed a few years back in the visitor's centre of the brewery, and since then have been used to mature the Bush. The result after bottling is *Bush Grand Prestige*, an exceptionally original beer that can create its own cults!

Bush Grand Prestige 13% vol. alc.

BREWED BY   Brasserie Dubuisson, Pipaix

STYLE   amber-coloured regional beer

BEN'S TASTING NOTES   an aroma of Bourbon whiskey, vanilla from the oak; at the same time sweet (from the alcohol) and dry (from the tannins in the wood); a very intense beer with a very long finish

FOOD PAIRING   try this some time with blue cheese!

CHIMAY CINQ CENTS   TRAPPIST

This is the 75 cl version of the *capsule blanche* ('white cap'), that is to say, Chimay's blond triple. All right, it is a perhaps a little confusing, but the real beer experts know what it is. This beer is perhaps the most underestimated triple in Flanders, because it is not yet really known there. A few years ago the good fathers risked bringing out the beer in barrel, too, after a second fermentation. A bold move, and the resulting product is well worth tasting in one of the twenty outlets for this barrel beer in Belgium.

Chimay Cinq Cents 8% vol. alc.

BREWED BY Abbaye Notre-Dame de Scourmont, Chimay

STYLE triple trappist beer

BEN'S TASTING NOTES spicy and bitter aroma with touches of clove and curaçao; dry and fruity, with a warm alcoholic and also bitter finish

FOOD PAIRING monkfish with cream sauce and grey shrimps

CHIMAY GRANDE RÉSERVE   TRAPPIST

Chimay, in the impoverished south of the province of Hainault, accommodates one of the world's most famous trappist-brewing monasteries, the Abbaye de Notre-Dame de Scourmont. As soon as you enter the town you are conscious of it, because of the brew-kettle which stands on the roundabout. The trappist brewery has been there for more than 150 years.

There are three beers in their range: the red cap (brown), white cap (triple) and blue cap (a strong brown). The *Grande Reserve* is the 75 cl offering of the darkest and heaviest Chimay. In a big bottle the beer is even softer than in a 33 cl bottle. It is one of my favourite beers, and always a winner at my tasting evenings. But did you know that it is also the perfect companion for a good Havana cigar? It is the strong, smoky and malty touches and the hop-bitter finish that can serve as a counter to the aromas of leather, wood and chocolate in a good Havana. An ideal beer to get you through the winter and, served in the glow of a crackling open fire, it reconciles you with life again.

Chimay Grande Réserve 9% vol. alc.

BREWED BY Abbaye Notre-Dame de Scourmont, Chimay

STYLE dark trappist beer

BEN'S TASTING NOTES bitter chocolate on the nose, spicy, sweet beginning with a surprisingly bitter finish

FOOD PAIRING spicy game dishes

CORSENDONK AGNUS AND PATER

ABBEY BEERS

Corsendonk abbey beer was launched some twenty-six years ago by Jef Keersmaekers, a beer merchant in Turnhout, at the peak of the recovery period for special beer. Jef has done well with this beer, which is completely brewed for him at brasserie Du Bocq in Purnode, which specializes in contract brewing of this type. The packaging with the decorative logo of the Corsendonk Priory looks

attractive, and particularly the elegant goblets filled with blond *Agnus*, or the darker *Pater*, appeal strongly to beer lovers in these regions. The taste of the beer is excellent, the Du Bocq people know their trade, and Jef looks after the marketing and distribution with his two sons, Michel and Stefaan. A good example of Campine entrepreneurship. In 2006 they celebrated the centenary of Keersmaekers Brewery, which brewed their own Pater beer until the 1960s.

Corsendonk Agnus 9% vol. alc.

BREWED BY Brouwerij Du Bocq, Purnode (for Brouwerij Keersmaekers)

STYLE triple abbey beer

BEN'S TASTING NOTES golden blond colour; spicy nose with aromas of fresh cream; slightly sweet taste with a hint of citrus and a fairly bitter finish

FOOD PAIRING asparagus à la Flamande

Corsendonk Pater 7,5% vol. alc.

BREWED BY Brouwerij Du Bocq, Purnode (for Brouwerij Keersmaekers)

STYLE dark abbey beer

BEN'S TASTING NOTES mild smell with aromas of caramel, malt, yeast and spices; fairly sweet initial taste which goes on to a slightly bitter finish

FOOD PAIRING steak with a cream and mushroom sauce

DE KONINCK SPÉCIALE BELGE

I have lived in Antwerp since my student days, and without being chauvinistic I dare to say that when you are very thirsty nothing beats a '*bolleke*', a typical goblet of freshly drawn De Koninck. It is a little bit sour and tart, but that makes the beer so fresh and drinkable. And then there's that deep amber colour; the hand-thrown round glass on a foot. There's also that 'German style' of tapping the beer in two or three goes, and the association with those real brown Antwerp pubs, where a *bolleke* still tastes best.

Modeste van den Bogaert, who ran the brewery at the time, is still alive and is now in his eighties. His sons, Dominique and Bernard carry on the business, and hopefully they will not fall into the hands of some giant company or other. The Antwerper puts his *bolleke* at the same level as Rubens, the Cathedral, the Steen, Antwerp's delicious fashion, and their liqueur, 'Elixir d'Anvers'. Their glass of beer is equated with Antwerp and that is no small beer for such a great city. I always think it tastes best in De Engel at the Grote Markt.

De Koninck 5% vol. alc.

BREWED BY Brouwerij De Koninck, Antwerp

STYLE spéciale Belge

BEN'S TASTING NOTES bitter yeast and hop in the nose, complemented with fruity touches, mainly banana; the beer has a great deal of body (it has not been fermented out too much) and takes its character from the yeast and the Saaz hop; a long and bitter finish

FOOD PAIRING savoury meat dishes

DELIRIUM TREMENS   STRONG BLOND BEER

In Melle near Ghent there is still one brewery left to uphold the reputation of Ghent in this respect. It is the Huyghe brewery, which has now been established for 352 years. Until 1985 mainly *Golden Kenia Pils* was brewed there for the local cafés, until son-in-law Jean de Laet changed tack and began to brew special beers in the full recovery period of special beer (1986 was the year of the beer). First came an amber-coloured type, the Artevelde, but this beer did not do so well, because of the brilliant success of Palm in that period. Later they did hit the bull's-eye with *Delirium Tremens*, a blond top fermentation beer with a high alcohol content and packed in a special mat-sprayed white bottle with a blue label and pink elephants. A little odd, as the name suggests. *Delirium Tremens* is, after all, Latin for a very advanced state of drunkenness. De Laet later also created a 'Confrérie van de Roze Olifant', the Brotherhood of the Pink Elephant, which could be admired once a year on the opening night of the 'Beer Passion Weekend' in June. Many prominent citizens of Antwerp, Ludo van Campenhout and Philip Heylen (aldermen) among them, have a blue and pink medal in their cupboard to show for it.

Delirium Tremens 9% vol. alc.

BREWED BY Brouwerij Huyghe, Melle
STYLE strong blond beer
BEN'S TASTING NOTES herby nose (fennel, aniseed, liquorice); round and warm alcoholic taste, yet with a little bitterness in the finish
FOOD PAIRING grilled salmon or pasta carbonara

DEUS BRUT DES FLANDRES   BIÈRE BRUT

Deus, the Latin for God, and also the name of a well-known Belgian pop group, has for some years also meant a beer, and not just any old beer. 'Other beers might approach but no beer can match the delicacy of a Deus' is what the late Michael Jackson had to say of it, and other international beer experts, too, go into raptures at their first tasting of this original beer. The presentation is spectacular too: an elegant reproduction of an antique champagne bottle, with a label looking discreetly aristocratic. The Bosteels family of brewers actually live in a small château in the middle of the village of Bruggenhout, and 'noblesse oblige'. They worked for a long time on this beer, which they call 'a drink for the gods, based on barley', and in full is described as *Deus Brut des Flandres*, *Cuvée Prestige*. So it looks like champagne, full of bubbles and blond in colour, but... it also has a head! The head is creamy like a meringue, with perfect saturation.

Deus leaves no beer lover unmoved, and I often let it be the last beer to be tasted at my beer tastings. The reactions are always overwhelming: 'A fragrant aroma, flowers, herbs, melts on the tongue… warm alcoholic and very dry finish… I've never drunk anything like it before.'

You can also combine Deus with dishes to your heart's delight. Chef Paul Mariën of the 'Truffeltje' in Dendermonde once prepared oysters with green herbs to go with it for us, and recently Jan and Frans Lamberechts of ''t Ebdiep' restaurant in Sint-Amands combined it with a fresh pasta with Ossobuco and Cecina de León. Deus – always served very cold from the ice bucket – is a brilliant aperitif and also a digestif and combines very well with a fresh summer dish. Cheers!

Deus Brut des Flandres 12% vol. alc.

BREWED BY Brouwerij Bosteels, Buggenhout

BEN'S TASTING NOTES Aroma: very complex and spicy aroma with hints of thyme, ginger, mint, lemon balm, and much more. In the taste the same herbal touches return, supplemented with a light sweetness of the alcohol; the strong injection of carbon dioxide tickles the tongue and palate and makes the beer refreshing, and it gives an enormous delicacy to this nonetheless strong beer. The finish is long, intense and refreshing.

FOOD PAIRING ideal with oysters

DOUBLE ENGHIEN   REGIONAL BEER

In the small Hainault village of Silly (always a source of amusement in English!), between Enghien and Ath, you can still find a typical farm-brewery from times past. The Van der Haegen-Meynsbrughe family has been wielding the stirrer there for four generations, and it will soon be the turn of the fifth. Silly is known particularly for its *saison* beer so typical of the region. But in 1975 the Tennstedt-Decroes brewery in neighbouring Enghien was taken over, so it added the popular *Double Enghien* to its range. This is an interesting *bière de garde*. No refermentation, blond and with a peppery hop aroma; it sometimes reminds you a little of a light Duvel. A quite special and original beer, almost unknown in Flanders, but more than worth discovering.

Double Enghien Blonde 7,5% vol. alc.

BREWED BY	Brasserie de Silly, Silly
STYLE	blond regional beer
BEN'S TASTING NOTES	herbs and fine hops dominate the aroma; the taste is full, with a sour, tickling sensation on the tongue and a dry, bitter finish
FOOD PAIRING	it goes well with a savoury hotpot

DRIE FONTEINEN OUDE GEUZE

SPONTANEOUS FERMENTATION

A few years ago in the Payotten country Armand De Belder started brewing lambic beer again in Beersel. He had earlier let lambic mature in the old '*foeders*' (large wooden tuns) of his late father, Gaston, a geuze brewer and manager of the Drie Fonteinen restaurant in the market place in Beersel. Armand is a great champion of traditionally made geuze and decided that he ought to make his basic beer himself. For that he bought old wooden tuns from the Pilsner Urquel brewery in the Czech Republic (which had switched to stainless steel), and began brewing a few houses down the road from the restaurant.

His *Drie Fonteinen Oude Geuze* and *Oude Kriek* have meanwhile developed into icons of the art of brewing lambic. You can't find these beers everywhere, so your best bet is to go and collect them from Armand's shop. Or you can try them with a tasty sandwich of pot cheese and radishes, a good hotpot, or a serving of mussels in the restaurant of the same name, which is now run by his brother.

Drie Fonteinen Oude Geuze 6% vol. alc.

BREWED BY Brouwerij-geuzestekerij Drie Fonteinen, Beersel

STYLE oude geuze

BEN'S TASTING NOTES a hint of Granny Smith apples in the nose; an intense taste, a combination of a well-balanced fresh sourness and nutlike bitterness

FOOD PAIRING ideal as an aperitif on a hot summer's afternoon, also good with mussels

DUCHESSE DE BOURGOGNE

MIXED FERMENTATION

Duchesse de Bourgogne from Vichte in West Flanders is a fine and thirst-quenching beer from a mixed fermentation. The beer is called after Maria, the daughter of the Duke of Burgundy, who was born in Bruges in 1457. When she became duchess, she looked after the interests of the Flemish people. Her beautiful picture, a little Flemish primitive, is proudly displayed on the large, decorative bottle. The Verhaeghe brewery in Vichte is one of the breweries in south-west Flanders specializing in old brown beer, so a beer of mixed fermentation. That is a top-fermented beer which has matured for between eight and eighteen months in oak barrels, so that it produces a lactic acid which gives the beer a fruity and sour complexity. The tannins of the oak ensure a woody, wine-like and dry taste. Well-known examples of this style of beer include Rodenbach, Petrus Oud Bruin and Bacchus. They are very complex beers, and as in all beers a good balance is important. Duchesse de Bourgogne has the ideal balance between sweet and sour

and is therefore very drinkable and at the same time very refreshing in hot weather. Michael Jackson himself spoke of 'a very interesting interplay of passion-fruit and chocolate'. The splendid bottle is silk-screen printed so that the label does not come off when you put the bottle in a cold ice bucket.

Duchesse de Bourgogne 6,2% vol. alc.

BREWED BY Brouwerij Verhaeghe, Vichte

STYLE Flemish reddish brown beer

BEN'S TASTING NOTES very like wine, with wood, cherries and almonds; fruity and even sweet at the end with an ice-cream-like touch of vanilla; very refreshing

FOOD PAIRING sour dishes like herring or ceviche (escabeche)

Duchesse de Bourgogne

DUVEL STRONG BLOND BEER

If you drive from Antwerp to Brussels along the A 12 you can't pass the Breendonk exit without seeing the white façade, inscribed in red letters: 'ssst... hier rijpt den Duvel' (shush... the Duvel is maturing here). Here are the maturing cellars of Duvel Moortgat, where thousands of crates of Duvel are stored and are continuing to ferment at an average temperature of 21°C. This is in fact the final fermentation in bottle, which provides the fruity esters in the beer, and this fermentation can last as long as three weeks. After that the beer goes on developing in the bottle, and some beer lovers enthuse about Duvel which has been kept for at least a year in their own cellar. In ¡Foodie! Beer, however, it is drunk young, when it is in fact considered to be at its best. It is a beer of character, but because of its pale colour (pils malt is used for it) and its sparkle, with a good, thick head, it looks like a very easily drinkable beer. Many a foreigner has been carried off after knocking back too much Duvel, because it is a very

treacherous beer, with 8.5 degrees of alcohol; it goes down very smoothly and fast, particularly when served cold in that handsome, tall Duvel glass which has become a real icon in the world of special beers. The typical 'spritz' on the tongue (Duvel prickles particularly on the tongue) you will not find in any other beer.

The fact is that Duvel has an enormous success on the market, and can still report doubled figures for growth every year. The Moortgat family floated the business on the stock exchange a few years ago, and is now assured of a sound capital structure to launch their Duvel across the whole world as one of the world classics of Belgian beer. The Flemish singer Paul Michiels is an enthusiastic fan and once called it 'the Beatles of beer'. We drink to that!

Duvel 8,5% vol. alc.

BREWED BY	Brouwerij Duvel-Moortgat, Breendonk
STYLE	strong blond beer
BEN'S TASTING NOTES	strong hoppy nose with good prickle on the tongue; refreshing and very digestible, the Poire Williams among beers
FOOD PAIRING	prawns in a creamy cocktail sauce

ENAME TRIPEL   ABBEY BEER

In the East Flanders town of Oudenarde, the Roman brewery, best known for its local brown beer and its Romy Pils, could not ignore the growing success of abbey beers, and in the 1990s it developed its own range of Ename abbey beers, called after the historic site of an abbey in the village of Ename, close to Mater, where the brewery is situated. Jozef Snauwaert, the master brewer, one of the best brewers in Belgium, with thirty-five years experience, could let himself go and worked on the product for several years: eventually *Ename Bruin*, *Blond* and *Tripel* reached the market. These beers are doing well in export, but also locally, since the brewery still has a strong patrimony of tied cafés. The management is now in the hands of the young generation, Lode and Carlo Roman. In 2007 they actually won the title of *Meester van de Gerst* (Master of the Barley) from *Beer Passion Magazine* for the modern management with which they lead this centuries-old family business, established in 1545.

Ename Tripel 9% vol. alc.

BREWED BY	Brouwerij Roman, Oudenarde
STYLE	triple abbey beer
BEN'S TASTING NOTES	fruity aroma with touches of honey, orange and peach; very complex beer with a light, refreshing bitter taste at the end
FOOD PAIRING	semi-hard abbey cheese

GOUDEN CAROLUS CLASSIC REGIONAL BEER

No one will ever forget their first Gouden Carolus. I drank mine in Leuven's Oude Markt, in De Kroeg, the café where militants (I'm talking of 1973) kept going until the morning. What always struck me at the time was that the message on the bottle, then still printed, announced that the shelf-life of this beer was unlimited.

The Van Breedam family from Mechelen has brewed this monument among Belgian beers since 1960, and until midway through the seventies, this beer, together with Duvel and the trappists, was virtually the only special beer. But with the advent of the tidal wave of special beers Gouden Carolus lost this position. The beer lapsed into obscurity and was even brewed and distributed by third parties, until Charles Leclef, a cousin of the Van Breedams, put his shoulder to it in 1998. He gradually rebuilt the old Het Anker brewery (a museum in itself) and in 1999 came up with a *Cuvée van de*

Gouden Carolus Classic 8,5% vol. alc.

BREWED BY	Brouwerij Het Anker, Mechelen
STYLE	strong dark beer
BEN'S TASTING NOTES	caramel sweet and slightly burnt aroma, and a herbal touch of coriander and plenty of fruit; with a lovely balance between sweet and (burnt) bitter and a light acerbity, this is a beer with a very complete taste; the finish is long and fruity
FOOD PAIRING	chocolate mousse made with real Callebaut chocolate

Keizer, a heavier variety. Still later *Gouden Carolus Triple* and *Ambrio* came on the market.

The beers are all of exceptional quality and have won many international prizes. Charles Leclef has a tenacious staying power, and it is thanks to people like him that our rich brewing culture survives.

Gouden Carolus Triple 9% vol. alc.

BREWED BY Brouwerij Het Anker, Mechelen

STYLE triple regional beer

BEN'S TASTING NOTES aroma and taste interspersed with tropical fruit and herbs, intense and powerful taste, again with tropical accents such as banana and figs

FOOD PAIRING rabbit, pork, cassoulet, grilled squid

Gouden Carolus Classic

GRIMBERGEN BLOND   ABBEY BEER

Grimbergen is an abbey beer that has been around for a long time; in the 1950s the Maes brewery made a deal for it with the Norbertine abbey of Grimbergen. This abbey had been destroyed several times in its history, hence the emblem on the label of a phoenix, which always rises from the ashes. Little is now left of the abbey, but the former abbey church in the centre of Grimbergen is breathtaking. In the nearby Fenikshof you can also visit a small museum that is devoted to beer.

Originally there was only Grimbergen brown or double, and it must be said, when drawn from the barrel I always found this beer particularly good. With the success of blond abbey beers flowing over the border from France, a blond version could naturally not be far behind.

Did you know that today Grimbergen is mainly promoted to go with food? It is the trendy beer and food pairing that is recommended in today's brasseries and restaurants. The whole Grimbergen range obviously tastes particularly good with the typical brasserie cuisine, the words of Michael Jackson suggesting that the beer is at least as complex as wine, if not more so.

Grimbergen Blond 6,7% vol. alc.

BREWED BY	Brouwerij Alken-Maes, Alken
STYLE	blond abbey beer
BEN'S TASTING NOTES	predominantly fruity nose (green bananas, hence fresh); fairly sweet in the middle area; the finish is short and slightly bitter
FOOD PAIRING	ideal with a creamy fish dish

GROTTENBIER REGIONAL BEER

Who doesn't know Pierre Celis? In his old age this 'godfather of white beer' had a brilliant idea which, among other things, inspired the brewers of brut beers. What he wanted to do was to let a specialist beer mature in caves, like champagne. His project could not at first go ahead because of administrative problems with the local government in Walloon Brabant, where the caves were that he had his eyes on. Eventually he found the marlstone caves in Kanne, near Maastricht, where he could do what he had so long wanted to do, to store the bottles in champagne racks and tilting and turning them to let the yeast settle at a constant temperature (although he did not employ the *rémuage* and *dégorgement* method as well). The beer was launched in 1998. An article was devoted to it in the first *Beer Passion Magazine*. This beer is today brewed at St Bernard's in Watou; the first brews came from De Smedt. Maturing is now also done in the caves at Valkenburg (the Netherlands). It is particularly Pierre's secret mixture of herbs and the special maturing that makes this beer so unique. Especially abroad (America) *Grottenbier* has become a true cult object.

Grottenbier 6,5% vol. alc.

BREWED BY	Brouwerij Sint-Bernardus, Watou (Pierre Célis' recipe)
STYLE	dark regional beer
BEN'S TASTING NOTES	full and malty bouquet; the taste is reminiscent of caramel and honey; the finish is slightly medicinal, resinous and very long
FOOD PAIRING	savoury stew of beef or lamb

GULDEN DRAAK REGIONAL BEER

The heaviest beer of the Van Steenberge brewery in Ertvelde is called after the famous golden dragon on the Ghent Belfort, and there is a story behind this. The dragon (which has no feet) clearly refers to a Viking ship. The origin of the dragon is in fact the story of a Norman king who ordered the sculpture to put in front of the cathedral of Constantinople. After that the carving came home to Ghent with the crusaders. The beer is very sturdy, sweet and strong and would indeed have satisfied the Vikings' taste. The special packaging – a bottle sprayed white and a black label with a golden dragon and red lettering – is rather kitsch, but there's still something to it.

Gulden Draak 10,5% vol. alc.

BREWED BY	Brouwerij Van Steenberge (Bios), Ertvelde
STYLE	strong dark beer
BEN'S TASTING NOTES	this reddish-brown knockout beer has plenty of sweetness from the alcohol, and the toasted malts makes it a real winter warmer
FOOD PAIRING	in and with goulash, but also delicious with a dark chocolate gateau

HAPKIN STRONG BLOND BEER

In Houtland in West Flanders, between Courtrai and Bruges, the Louwaege brewery brewed pils and special beers until a few years ago. Their best beer was Hapkin, which was launched in 1982 as the counterpart of Duvel in their own cafés. The name comes from a count of Flanders, Baldwin Hapkin, who once galloped around menacingly waving an axe. You can still find the axe on the label, together with two brewers with raised stirring rods. My first design project as a marketing consultant in 1992! However, *Hapkin* could do little against the overwhelming success of Duvel, not even when Louwaege was taken over a few years later by Alken-Maes and *Hapkin* got free access to all their cafés. Where Alken-Maes does deserve praise is the way in which they moved the production of Hapkin to their own brewery. This was done with great care and respect for all aspects, so that you can taste little difference in the rich taste of this strong blond beer.

Technically it compares very well in taste with Duvel, and some beer lovers even think it is better, thanks to its higher spread of bitterness.

Just try it some time, it is in all respects a beer that deserves more attention.

Hapkin 8,5% vol. alc.

BREWED BY	Brouwerij Alken-Maes, Alken
STYLE	strong blond beer
BEN'S TASTING NOTES	golden yellow with a thick head; herbal and hoppy, rounded and soft, with a long, dry finish
FOOD PAIRING	a good steak au *poivre* goes very well with it

HOEGAARDEN   WHITE BEER

The story of Pierre Célis, the milkman who in the 1960s breathed new life into the centuries-old Hoegaarden white beer, is well known. Célis started brewing in one of his wife's cut-down wash tubs and was quickly successful with his sweetish-sour white beer, particularly in student circles. The beer was so popular that in the 1980s he could no longer meet the demand. When in his absence (he was travelling to the USA) the brewery caught fire and was burnt down, big brother Interbrew jumped in to help the brewery up again. Célis moved to Texas and Interbrew became Inbev. The peak of *Hoegaarden Witbier*'s success was around the 1990s, after which consumption declined, to the advantage of abbey and fruit beers. However, in export the beer still always does well, and these days it is even very fashionable in London not to have a white wine with your meal, but a 'Hoegaarden White'.

Hoegaarden 5% vol. alc.

BREWED BY	Brouwerij De Kluis, Hoegaarden
STYLE	white beer
BEN'S TASTING NOTES	aroma of coriander and orange peel; also in the taste a perfect balance between freshness and sweetness; a refreshing thirst-quencher in summer
FOOD PAIRING	good with sardines and salmon, but also with turbot

KASTEEL BRUIN & TRIPEL   REGIONAL BEER

When I tasted this beer for the first time in the late 1980s, the aroma made me think of freshly sliced bread. You never forget these first impressions. Brewer Luc van Honsebrouck is one of Belgium's most colourful brewers, to quote Michael Jackson. And he ought to know: during a visit Van Honsebrouck let him taste seven vintages of the strong *Kasteelbier* and then asked: 'Will you come to my funeral when I die?' This brewer-chatelain from Ingelmunster

always knows how to couple good brewing practice with original ideas, and is also well able to sell his beer. *Kasteelbier Bruin* and *Blond*, recently rechristened *Kasteel Bruin* and *Tripel*, were a shot in the bull's eye. They are beers which are in no sense copies, but are very much their own (strong) selves. *Kasteel Bruin* is a class apart. *Kasteel Tripel* can stand comparison with the best triples in the country.

Kasteel Bruin 11% vol. alc.

BREWED BY	Brouwerij Van Honsebrouck, Ingelmunster
STYLE	strong dark regional beer
BEN'S TASTING NOTES	aroma of freshly sliced bread; rich taste reminiscent of port; sweet, fruity, herbal and a reasonably bitter finish
FOOD PAIRING	foie gras, Stilton cheese, crème brulée

Kasteel Tripel 11% vol. alc.

BREWED BY	Brouwerij Van Honsebrouck, Ingelmunster
STYLE	strong blond regional beer
BEN'S TASTING NOTES	sweetish nose with touches of hops; slightly herbal, predominantly tasting of esters with penetrating bitterness
FOOD PAIRING	ideal with lobster and bouillabaisse

Kasteelbier Bruin & Tripel

KEIZER KAREL RUBY RED   REGIONAL BEER

From the year 2000, when the quincentenary of the birth of the emperor Charles V (Keizer Karel) was celebrated, the Haacht brewery in Boortmeerbeek has had this dark beer on the market. You would associate a powerful and prominent beer with a name like that, so Van Haacht's brewmasters came up with a slightly dry dark beer with a strong, soft, rounded feel in the mouth. There is a hint of liquorice and it has a warm finish. The beer is sometimes drunk from a ceramic beaker with three handles, a reminder of the well-known story of the pot with three handles from Olen. Recently a blond version with 8.5% vol. alc. has also been available.

Keizer Karel Ruby Red 7% vol. alc.

BREWED BY	Brouwerij Haacht, Boortmeerbeek
STYLE	ruby red regional beer
BEN'S TASTING NOTES	strong and soft, full-bodied taste; with touches of liquorice and a warm finish
FOOD PAIRING	steaks and grills

LA CHOUFFE   REGIONAL BEER

For twenty-five years Chris Bauweraerts and his brother-in-law Pierre Gobron have been brewing their *La Chouffe* ('the Gnome') in the Ardennes village of Achouffe near Houffalize. From the start this unusual beer (only available in 75 cl bottles) was a success, but it can't be classified in any specific category. The gnomes on the packaging make it very appealing, and the beer is well merchandized. The combination of the original taste and the well promoted marketing works extremely well. This was also clear to Duvel-Moortgat, who took over Chris and Pierre's little brewery in 2006, when they were faced with succession problems. But with Duvel they are sitting comfortably.

La Chouffe 8% vol. alc.

BREWED BY	Brasserie d'Achouffe, Achouffe-Wibrin
STYLE	blond regional beer
BEN'S TASTING NOTES	malty and fruity aroma; the taste is herbal with predominantly citrus fruits; the hop is from Saaz, and only one spice is added: coriander
FOOD PAIRING	refreshing salads and salmon dishes

LEFFE BLOND ABBEY BEER

The same age as your humble servant. In 1952 this abbey beer first saw the light as a result of a coincidence: Albert Lootvoet, a brewer from Overijse, was dining with the abbot of the Norbertine abbey of Leffe (Dinant), who was complaining that their income was insufficient to maintain the abbey. Lootvoet suggested brewing a beer for them under licence, and the rest is history. Lootvoet later sold his brewery to Artois. Leffe is now brewed in Leuven by the mighty Inbev and has become a global brand. It appears to lead all Belgian abbey beers in export.

It is not surprising that *Leffe Blond* is the beer turning over most in volume. It shows a nice blond colour in its fine glass goblet; with its 6.5 degrees it is still reasonably easy to drink, and it is therefore a threat to all special, easily drinkable, beers. Your humble servant saw that clearly in 1989, and he launched the beer in all Inbev cafés, against the wishes of his superiors, who swore by the brown abbey beer, which showed up well in the market studies.

Sometimes you are right, but you don't always get it right. Today this blond abbey beer is the most popular one, even the Trappists of Westmalle now sell more triple than double. So in the end I was proved right after all!

Leffe Blond 6,5% vol. alc.

BREWED BY	InBev, Leuven
STYLE	blond abbey beer
BEN'S TASTING NOTES	sunny colour; light herbal aroma; restrained orangey fruitiness and a light, dry finish
FOOD PAIRING	try this with rosé-cooked tuna steak with a soy sauce

Leffe Blond

LIEFMANS GOUDEN BAND MIXED FERMENTATION

The showpiece of the Liefmans brewery is undoubtedly the *Gouden Band* (Golden Riband). The beer is even available in two versions: one which has undergone refermentation in the bottle and one that has not, intended for export. Belgians can easily cope with the more complex tastes, so we drink the refermented version. The beer has for some time been brewed in Dentergem (Riva brewery took over Liefmans in 1990), but is still finished in the Oudenarde installations, which have been in the business since 1679. It is like visiting a grand museum. The process consists of the typical fermentation in open vats in which the wort (the mixture supplied by Dentergem) is exposed to the wind. When the beer has finished fermenting, it is stored in the brewery's cool cellars. It rests there for many months, until it is mixed with older beer. This typical mixed fermentation in Oudenarde should be protected, just like the traditional *mattentaarten*, sweet pastries from Geraardsbergen!

Liefmans Gouden Band 8% vol. alc.

BREWED BY Liefmans Breweries, brewed in Dentergem, fermented and finished in Oudenarde

BEN'S TASTING NOTES malty and herbal; rich in esters, so that the nose is very fruity; tingling fresh on the tongue; fine balance between the lactic acid touch and the sweetness of the toasted malt, very balanced and complex beer; the finish is long and slightly sour

FOOD PAIRING goat's cheese, pickles

Liefmans Gouden Band

LIEFMANS KRIEK MIXED FERMENTATION

This is really a pearl in Belgium's beer culture. And also an odd one.

How does the production process go? The basic sour Liefmans beer from the mixed fermentation is taken and pumped into the big settling tanks of the Oudenarde site. In this tank are tons of Belgian and Danish cherries. The beer is, as it were, put on top, and this starts up a unique maceration process (soaking) that may well last six months, in which thirteen kilos of cherries is needed for a hundred litres of beer. Afterwards it is 're-assembled' with a mixture of young (six months old) beer. That is how you get the phenomenal taste of *Liefmans Kriek*.

It is a very labour-intensive process, in which the brewer has to spread the cherries out by hand in the long, horizontal, shallow tanks. Afterwards the skins and the cherry stones also have to be removed by hand. But the results are excellent.

Liefmans Kriek 6% vol. alc.

BREWED BY Brouwerij Liefmans, Oudenarde

STYLE kriek (cherry) based on old brown beer

BEN'S TASTING NOTES aromas of cherries, wood, almonds and caramel; sour sweetish approach; good acidity produces a refreshing taste

FOOD PAIRING in a zabaglione and combined with meat loaf and northern cherries

LINDEMANS CUVÉE RENÉ AND KRIEK

SPONTANEOUS FERMENTATION

When I first met René Lindemans in his farm brewery in Vlezenbeek, he received me in his work apron and excused himself for having so little time, as he had to stoke up the kettle (with coal and wood) for the next brew. We are writing about the year 1984 and the little brewery then produced about five thousand hectolitres a year. Today Lindemans has become a big business, largely thanks to the success of its geuze and kriek (cherry) beers in America, and particularly from the launch of the 'sweet' *Lindemans Kriek* in the late 1970s. This Kriek is no longer made with real fruit, but with juice. It does the brewery no harm, and today you can find the most modern installations there, because the turnover runs to more than eighty thousand hectolitres.

One of the showpieces of the brewery is the *Cuvée René Grand Cru*, called after the brewer. On the small green 37.5 cl bottle a yellow ochre label shows up, entirely in art nouveau style. So a nice label, but what is in the bottle? A genuine

Lindemans Cuvée René and Kriek

old geuze, extremely suitable for drinking in hot sunny weather, as it is quite sour, but oh so thirst-quenching. It is a pity that this type of beer gets so little opportunity from beer lovers, who are increasingly switching to sweetness. This is after all what this country is great in: the oldest style of beer in the world (spontaneous fermentation), and nowadays only found in Belgium. Old geuze is unsweetened, the result of mixing old and young lambic, matured in oak casks. There are still about seven producers in the Payotten region, and we must cherish this treasury of beer.

Lindemans Kriek 3,5% vol. alc.

BREWED BY Brouwerij Lindemans, Vlezenbeek

STYLE kriek (cherry) beer based on lambic

BEN'S TASTING NOTES ripe apples in the nose, fairly round and sweet to start, with the cherry taste at the end

FOOD PAIRING zabaglione with cherries

Lindemans Cuvée René 5% vol. alc.

BREWED BY Brouwerij Lindemans, Vlezenbeek

STYLE old geuze

BEN'S TASTING NOTES aroma of white pepper and cedar wood; sweetish sour taste and very fruity, with a long dry finish

FOOD PAIRING good with prawns, ceviche (Peruvian fish dish)

MALHEUR BRUT RÉSERVE BIÈRE BRUT

Michael Jackson called the Belgian brewers 'the most idiosyncratic brewers in the world'. What did he mean? That they are the most stubborn and eccentric, always lusting after super-creative brews. And sometimes the 'beerhunter' took part in this game. For instance, we were once sitting round the bar of the Hippodroom restaurant in south Antwerp, having a chat with an American importer and with Manu De Lantsheer of Malheur Brewery in Buggenhout. 'Would there be a brewer in Belgium mad enough to make a beer by the traditional method of Dom Perignon, the inventor of champagne?' Michael wondered. To which the importer replied: 'If there was such a beer, I would immediately order a container load of it.' Manu De Landtsheer did not need to hear that a second time and went straight to work. He went on a study trip to Epernay and learnt all about *rémuage* and *dégorgement* from the champagne makers. He took his *Malheur 10* as a base, a strong blond and finely hopped beer, and bottled it in thick 75 cl champagne bottles with a special yeast collector. For this he had a mobile bottling installation specially transferred from Rheims. He invested in some 'giropalettes', special revolving palettes in which the bottles could mature further, while the yeast could do its work through the process of turning and revolving (in other words, being distributed over the whole bottle so that it was all assimilated into the beer and a sparkling, bubbling drink resulted). Once fermentation was finished, the necks of the bottles were frozen so that the collector with the yeast plug could be removed. A secret liquid was then added, the cork and the foil

cover put in place, and the *Malheur Brut Réserve* was ready: the first 'bière brut' in the world (we are writing about September 2001). Since then many container loads have followed, Manu won the prize for invention, and he also developed a *Malheur Dark Brut* and a *Cuvée Royale*.

Jackson invented the term *bière brut* and he devoted a whole chapter to this style of beer in the latest edition of *Great Belgian Beers* (2006). It was, after all, not long before a second bière brut arrived on the markets, and from the same village: *Deus Brut des Flandres* (see p. 90).

Malheur Brut Réserve 11% vol. alc.

BREWED BY Brouwerij De Landtsheer, Buggenhout

BEN'S TASTING NOTES in the aroma you can smell pure hop flowers, combined with the fruity nose of green apples (Granny Smith), which makes this highly alcoholic beer predominantly refreshing. The taste is further characterized by dryness, a pleasant bitterness and a touch of sweetness from the alcohol. The finish is long, very dry on the palate and pleasantly bitter.

FOOD PAIRING for the launch chef Jan Buytaert of De Bellefleur combined this beer with a tartare of tuna, garnished with caviare

MALHEUR 10 REGIONAL BEER

The small De Landtsheer brewery in Buggenhout has now been in existence for ten years. It was the grandson of the house, Manu De Landtsheer, who started up brewing operations again. His grandfather, who ran a large business selling drinks in the region round Dendermonde, had been the last brewer in the family. Manu could not resist it and installed a brand-new micro brewery with all its accoutrements. He called his beer *Malheur 10* after the local dialect word 'Malheurke', for a little accident. His beer is always nicely hoppy; Manu always swears by the real Saaz hops, the best in the world.

What a relief that there are still new brewers who fight against sweetening!

Malheur 10% vol. alc.

BREWED BY Brouwerij De Landtsheer, Buggenhout

STYLE dark blond beer

BEN'S TASTING NOTES dry and bitter aroma (Saaz hops); to start the taste is sweet, but quickly changes to a strong bitterness; a well-balanced beer with a dry finish

FOOD PAIRING salmon steak with a piquant, seasoned sauce

Malheur 10

MAREDSOUS 6 & 8   ABBEY BEER

Maredsous is one of the less well known abbey beers. At Duvel Moortgat all attention is, after all, centred on Duvel, and over the years Maredsous has perhaps lost out somewhat. Nonetheless these are excellent beers (as you might expect, with a brewery like that!) and they certainly deserve a high ranking among abbey beers. That is what the *Beer Passion* tasting panel thought: when in 1999 the panel organized a tasting of abbey beers, the Maredsous

beers came out on top. The abbey of Maredsous, south of Dinant, attracts numerous visitors who try out the delicious combination of their beer and the cheese of the same name there. *Maredsous 8* is the only brown beer in the range, and also the descendant of the first Maredsous beer which the monks had made by a small local brewery. As you probably know, in those days (the 1950s) all abbey beers were brown. It is only with the breakthrough of Leffe that the market was 'blonded'. It may well be that the brown Rochefort was the inspiration here. What they have in common with that beer is the very successful combination between the sweetness (of the toasted malt) and the fine bitterness of the hops. I think it's a splendid beer, which, when I drink it, I like to accompany with a fragrant Havana cigar, such as a Punch Punch. The *Maredsous 6* is a piquant amber-blond abbey beer which is very drinkable. The *Maredsous Tripel* is another story again: a herbal and fruity blond taste bomb on which a lot of work has been done. Particularly this last beer has many gastronomic qualities, both when added to sauces and as an accompanying drink.

Maredsous 6% vol. alc.

BREWED BY Brouwerij Duvel-Moortgat, Breendonk
STYLE amber-blond abbey beer
BEN'S TASTING NOTES refreshing dairy smell; fairly herbal initial taste, with slightly sweet touches, ending in a sour-bitter finish
FOOD PAIRING spicy, exotic dishes

Maredsous 8% vol. alc.

BREWED BY Brouwerij Duvel-Moortgat, Breendonk
STYLE dark abbey beer
BEN'S TASTING NOTES fruity aroma with hints of banana, malt and biscuit; light herbal taste with pleasant, light bitter finish
FOOD PAIRING spare ribs, ox cheeks, lamb cutlets

MORT SUBITE OUDE KRIEK

SPONTANEOUS FERMENTATION

A great deal of *kriek* (cherry beer) is drunk on the terraces in summer. But who knows the difference between old kriek, ordinary kriek, and extra sweet kriek? The small Geuze producers in the Payotten region still make old kriek, that is to say, based on 100 per cent lambic kriek (that is lambic on which cherries have lain for a whole year, after which there is still two months maturing in the bottle). The larger producers, such as Belle Vue (Inbev) and Mort Subite (Alken Maes) have concentrated on the sweetened krieks, which have been given extra cherry juice – there may still have been some lambic kriek in it, but that was mostly for show. The marketers for these groups even went a step further and made respectively a *Kriek Extra* and a *Kriek Extreme*, very sweet stuff at which the true beer lover turns up his nose. But it sells! Well now, Old Kriek is sourish and sharp, and therefore thirst-quenching. And while I am writing this, I am trying a *Mort Subite Oude Kriek*.

Yes, Alken-Maes have after two years production time bottled 75,000 bottles of this drink of the gods and put them on the market. I think this is splendid, a large group making such a cultural product, evidence of its courage and vision. With their sales figures they will not try to scale any drastic heights, but what a contribution to their reputation. *Mort Subite* now has three versions of their *kriek*, and I, of course, plead in favour of the *Oude Kriek*.

Mort Subite Oude Kriek 6,5% vol. alc.

BREWED BY Brouwerij Mort Subite, Kobbegem

BEN'S TASTING NOTES fairly closed aroma: only after a little while is the smell released; this verges towards the vat in which the kriek lambic fermented and matured, rather than to the cherries themselves; intense cherry taste, with sourness as the high note; total absence of bitterness; long and intense finish; spreads out.

FOOD PAIRING this beer goes perfectly with blue cheeses, such as Roquefort, Fourme d'Ambert, Stilton, Gorgonzola, or Pas de Bleu

ORVAL TRAPPIST

Orval is simply the best aperitif you can imagine. Bone dry, from the extravagantly used Styrian Goldings hop. I once visited the brewery in the Trappist monastery of Orval (a true shrine, where you can't just go in) and stood amazed at the large bags of hops which were soaking like teabags in the brew-kettles, to give the extra flavour of hops. After drinking *Orval* you could eat a horse, just like after an old geuze. And just like in an old geuze, there are brettanomyces (wild yeasts) in it. *Orval* makes your stomach receptive. *Orval* is the only beer that is brewed in the brewery and has been since the 1930s. Neither bottle nor glasses have ever changed in appearance. The then architect of the abbey, Henri Vaes, had designed them 'between the soup and the potatoes' and today the handsome skittle-shaped bottle still has a purple label with a trout holding a ring in its mouth, and the robust goblets with a turned foot are still in use. None of the good fathers would ever dream of changing anything. And there

are yet more certainties. The good fathers, of course, only let their beer leave the brewery after six months, in order to be sure that the yeast had finished doing its work in the bottle. As I write, I am, of course, drinking an *Orval* and, musing, remember one of the great moments of my beer career; on a visit to the abbey, brother Xavier took me to the abbey church, where he took his seat behind the organ. It then appeared he was a virtuoso on that instrument, and for fifteen minutes I enjoyed divine baroque music. *Orval* is without question our most emblematic beer.

Orval 6,2% vol. alc.

BREWED BY	Abbaye Notre-Dame d'Orval
STYLE	light amber trappist beer
BEN'S TASTING NOTES	although the bitterness is predominant, a slight acid touch is also perceptible; a pleasant bitter finish, typical of a beer high in hops
FOOD PAIRING	ideal as an aperitif

PALM SPÉCIALE   SPÉCIALE BELGE

In my biography you can read that I was working for Palm for four years. That was in the 1980s, when special beers were at the height of their recovery. Palm was then doing very well, and only seemed to grow, until at the end of the last century the bottom fell out and the seven lean years started. The market for beer always goes in cycles, and a mono product like Palm is, of course, very sensitive to it. Today, however, the picture looks quite different. Palm is again the figurehead of Brabant brewing culture. As well as the main brand, the business also has a wide range of special beers, brewed according to the four methods of fermentation, in an innovative system of drawing from the wood and 75 cl presentations. *Tapmaster*, *Master Beers* and *Old Masters* are powerful concepts with which from a mono product they have advanced to a multi-niche strategy. Palm Spéciale still represents the greatest volume in sales. The beer again sits in its old familiar goblet and again communicates with its sturdy working class market. Are seven fat years in prospect again?

Palm Spéciale 5% vol. alc.

(also in 75cl refermented and with 5,4% vol. alc.)

BREWED BY	Palm Breweries, Steenhuffel
STYLE	spéciale Belge
BEN'S TASTING NOTES	fruity fermentation aroma, malty and mellow like honey; fine aroma of Kentish hops produces a subtle harmony
FOOD PAIRING	goes well with traditional Flemish cuisine, for instance chicory and ham with a cheese sauce baked in the oven provides a delicious contrast with the softness of Palm.

PALM ROYALE SPÉCIALE BELGE

This heavier version of Spéciale Belge was brewed specially for the ninetieth birthday of Palm brewer Alfred Van Roy. His passion for the emphatically fruity fermentation of his personally selected Palm yeasts is given an extreme expression in *Palm Royale*. I tasted this beer for the first time at the press conference in the brewery's reception centre. It was crowded and nobody criticized the house… because the beer was so good. Several casks had been tapped and the beer foamed in torrents into the tall goblets.

This beer is also very handsome in appearance, with its royal blue label and elegant goblets. I consider it to be one of the greatest discoveries of recent years and forecast a great future for it.

Palm Royale 7,5% vol. alc.

BREWED BY	Palm Breweries, Steenhuffel
STYLE	strong spéciale Belge
BEN'S TASTING NOTES	aroma of bananas, full in the mouth and plenty of body; slightly sweet from the alcohol, the beer is at the same time slightly bitter and fruity; the refermentation ensures a pleasant, dry finish
FOOD PAIRING	il once tried it with scampi and curry sauce; the mild beer made an amusing contrast with it

PATER LIEVEN BLOND ABBEY BEER

There is a whole story behind this beer. Ignace Van den Bossche, a brewer from Sint-Lievens-Esse, had seen the start of a Pater Lieven fifty years ago (he is himself in his late fifties) in the family brewery, on the occasion of the local St Livinus festival. It was an amber-coloured beer, not so high in alcohol, and could be drunk with pils when rounds were handed out. Times change, and by the early nineties nobody was interested in it any more. Ignace had the name, but not the beers that were doing so well – abbey beers! It was one of my first commissions as a marketing consultant. I advised Ignace to bring out a blond, a brown and a triple under the *Pater Lieven* brand name, and to adjust the label. We put a stylized brewing monk on it and… this appeared to be the saving of the brewery. Van den Bossche, now assisted by his two sons, is doing golden business abroad with his abbey beers. He still does everything himself, from breaking up the malt to bottling, and you can taste that: perhaps one of the best ranges of abbey beer in Belgium.

Pater Lieven Blond 6,5% vol. alc.

BREWED BY Brouwerij Van den Bossche, St.Lievens-Esse (Herzele)

STYLE blond abbey beer

BEN'S TASTING NOTES refreshing and creamy aromas, 'crackling' (from the malt), dry, slightly salty and very tasty

FOOD PAIRING eel in a cream sauce

PAUWEL KWAK REGIONAL BEER

Kwak is best known for its grand glass in its wooden stand, called a 'coachman's glass'. The Bosteels brewery has been sitting on a long tradition with this amber-coloured beer. They even call it a 'historic beer', but the glass is better known than the beer. The name *Kwak* refers to Pauwel Kwak, who brewed beer in Napoleonic times and specially designed this glass for the coachmen, who by the new Code Napoleon could not get down from the box when they stopped with their coach at an inn. They could hang this 'stirrup glass' on their coach, so that they did not suffer from thirst. In many cafés today, when you order a *Kwak*, you have to hand in a shoe as security for the glass. It looks spectacular, a *Kwak* served in this way. Personally I particularly like its unusually deep amber colour, which you hardly ever find elsewhere. I remember a ride in the Kwak coach with the Bosteels family through the old town centre of Bruges, with Michael Jackson. We attracted a great deal of attention with that coach, which was driven by two coachmen in traditional costume, with long capes

and top hats. Father Ivo Bosteels blew the horn, and regularly drank from his Kwak glass, which hung in its special holder. The coach stopped in front of the well-known Karmeliet restaurant, where we were treated to a magnificent lunch, richly accompanied, of course, by *Kwak* and *Tripel Karmeliet*. Unforgettable. The Bosteels family call themselves 'brewers of eccentric beers', and with their latest success, *Deus*, the herbal brut beer, they have crowned their eccentric operations.

Kwak drinks down very well, particularly when served from the barrel (relatively rarely). Be particularly careful of the last mouthful, because if you drink too fast, it will spill over your collar.

Pauwel Kwak 8% vol. alc.

BREWED BY	Brouwerij Bosteels, Buggenhout
STYLE	amber-coloured regional beer
BEN'S TASTING NOTES	soft sweetish nose with some herbs; malty taste and fully rounded in the mouth, with some bitterness in the finish
FOOD PAIRING	grilled meat dishes

PETRUS GOUDEN TRIPEL ABBEY BEER

The Bavik brewery in Bavikhove (Harelbeke) is a typical family brewery running a healthy business, with both feet on the ground and with traditional West-Flanders common sense. They work hard there, and every euro is turned over twice. I know these people very well from various marketing projects and they can be models for the 'hardworking Fleming', of that there is no doubt. They also make good beer which they distribute locally in a strong family chain of at least a thousand cafés, but also export, particularly to neighbouring northern France. Petrus is a flag that covers many cargoes; from old brown to blond, amber, double and triple, and recently also an 'aged pale', which is really the cream of the crop for real beer lovers. The *Petrus Gouden Tripel* is in my view their best beer, though in colour it is not as 'golden', but rather on the pale side. Well, you just have to accept that. The typical house yeast gives it that touch of acidity which makes all the special beers of the brewery so characteristic. They also

make one of the country's best pilsners, which has been singled out for distinctions many times.

The changing of the guard lies on the horizon for young Bert, who in a few years time will take over the torch from Ignace De Brabandere, who has gradually become a monument of brewing. While enjoying a good glass of wine, he has reached a friendly agreement with the owners of the famous Château Petrus about the use of the name. Petrus is here to stay.

Petrus Gouden Tripel 7,5% vol. alc.

BREWED BY	Brouwerij Bavik, Bavikhove
STYLE	triple abbey beer
BEN'S TASTING NOTES	the nose makes you think of pils; the taste is strong, but also fruity and yeasty
FOOD PAIRING	fillets of sole in saffron sauce

Petrus Gouden Tripel

POPERINGS HOMMELBIER   REGIONAL BEER

In the village of Watou, not far from Poperinghe and known for its annual poetry festival, there are still three breweries working with the local hops. One of them is the Van Eecke brewery, just beside the protected village green. With West-Flemish tenacity they go on brewing good hoppy beers there. The brewery's showpiece is Hommelbier, a name derived from the local dialect word 'hommel', meaning 'hop'. *Hommelbier* is brewed with no fewer than three different kinds of hop, and is described as a 'strong thirst-quencher'. A real taste bomb, which may make you change your mind if you are used to drinking sweet beers. And perhaps the taste for bitter beers is gradually coming back now that cola dispensers are increasingly being banned from schools. Real beer lovers go for bitter!

Poperings Hommelbier 7,5% vol. alc.

BREWED BY Brouwerij Van Eecke, Watou

STYLE strong blond regional beer

BEN'S TASTING NOTES hop, malt and a trickle of honey in the nose; the taste is strongly bitter and also reasonably malty; a splendid dry summer beer for the café terrace

FOOD PAIRING spicy oriental dishes

ROCHEFORT 8 TRAPPIST

The abbey of Notre Dame de Saint-Remy is perhaps the least known of the trappist breweries. It is situated close to the small town of Rochefort in the Famenne, a lovely stretch of country in the province of Namur. All three of the Rochefort beers are dark and on the sweet side. They were first brewed in 1595. The figures 5, 8 and 10 refer to the old system of degrees indicating the alcohol content. A *Rochefort 8* has eight 'old' degrees, but in current usage its percentage volume of alcohol is 9.2 per cent.

The abbey possesses one of the most beautiful brewhouses in the world, perhaps the most beautiful I have ever seen (and I have seen a few). High glass windows through which the sunlight shines in on the copper mixing vat and kettle, perfect lines and proportions, a thing of beauty. The beer should be too, it is always refermented in bottle and it tastes powerful and rich.

Rochefort 8 – 9,2% vol. alc.

BREWED BY	Abbaye Notre-Dame de Saint-Remy
STYLE	dark trappist beer
BEN'S TASTING NOTES	assertive palate of fruit (bananas, raisins), a hint of herbs; fairly sweet but not cloying; fairly dry, bitter finish. A complex and complete beer!
FOOD PAIRING	any dish with wild partridge

RODENBACH   MIXED FERMENTATION

Rodenbach beer from Roeselare is the burgundy among Belgian beers. It has a splendid red colour, but also the degree of acidity of this beer makes you think of wine. Precisely because of this sourness and sharpness in the taste it is very refreshing, and according to Michael Jackson even 'the world's most refreshing beer'.

Old posters in Roeselare proclaim as a slogan: 'it's wine'. The brewery is as old as the Belgian state, and its beer features on almost every menu in Belgium. On a visit to this brewery the gigantic oak tuns immediately strike the eye (see pp. 40-41). More than three hundred tuns are ranged in the galleries of Rodenbach, and their oak walls give the essential tannins to the basic beer, which is, among others, made with Viennese (red) malt. After the beer has rested for eighteen months to two years in wooden tuns, it is 100 per cent 'tun beer'. This is afterwards cut with young beer, proportionately 25 per cent old to 75 per cent young beer. Here we are talking about mixed fermentation, the maturing on oak causes microbiological activity which produces lactic and acetic acid in the beer. As the tuns are regularly scraped out inside, they can carry on doing their work. The brewery employs two coopers for their maintenance, in which numbered staves, hoops, reeds and beeswax are used.

The Rodenbach family, originally from Andernach (near Koblenz) founded the brewery in 1836. They produced famous sons, such as Alexander, a brewer and politician; Georges, and particularly Albrecht were great poets. When you go into the brewery, you see their statues standing there. You can then go into their handsome reception centre, dine among the storage tuns, and admire the portraits of the Rodenbach family.

Rodenbach is also a brilliant beer to combine with food. Food pairing is the latest trend in beer gastronomy, and the classic combination of *Rodenbach* with grey Ostend prawns and tomatoes remains highly recommended, particularly if you add a marinade of olive oil, white wine vinegar, and a dash of soya sauce.

Where the proportions in *Rodenbach* is one quarter old beer, that in *Rodenbach Grand Cru* is three-quarters. So that is a much more 'acid' beer, but also wields unexpected gastronomic trumps.

Rodenbach 5% vol. alc.

BREWED BY Brouwerij Rodenbach, Roeselare (part of Palm Breweries)

STYLE Flemish reddish brown beer

BEN'S TASTING NOTES refreshingly acid in the nose, sharp-tasting, fruity, also full in the mouth and fresh, with a slight reminiscence of sherry; good balance between sweet and sour, in which the lactic acid dominates the acetic; very refreshing and appetizing, with a mild finish

FOOD PAIRING classically with Ostend prawns

Rodenbach Grand Cru 6% vol. alc.

BREWED BY Brouwerij Rodenbach, Roeselare

STYLE Flemish reddish brown beer

BEN'S TASTING NOTES Complex beer with much wood and esters; vinous, and with an aroma of balsamic vinegar

FOOD PAIRING ceviche or escabeche, magnificent!

SAISON DUPONT SAISONS

The *saison* is a typical Walloon style of beer, characterized by hoppy and thirst-quenching beers. The style originated in the agricultural activities in the area around Tournai. When the workers came off the land during harvest time, they were very thirsty: a refreshing and hoppy beer awaited them, which was brewed in the same farm during the winter, when there was little work on the land.

Brasserie Dupont in Tourpes still brews a genuine *saison* with the colour of a pale pils, a herbal nose, and a strong bitterness with touch of acidity. In the brewery they still use direct fires to heat the kettles. The brewer swears by the old system, which warms up the mash and caramelizes the sugars, so that you get a fuller and richer beer. Hardly anyone does this now.

In the 'farmhouse brewery' cheese is also still made, and bread with the draff from the brew-kettle. All the beers from this brewery are more than worth trying. Dupont lives mainly from export.

Saison Dupont 6,5% vol. alc.

BREWED BY Brasserie Dupont, Tourpes

STYLE saison

BEN'S TASTING NOTES a little like white beer, slightly sourish, with a herbal nose and a bitter taste of hops

FOOD PAIRING ideal as an aperitif

Moinette Blonde 8,5% vol. alc.

BREWED BY Brasserie Dupont, Tourpes

STYLE saison

BEN'S TASTING NOTES citrus-like hoppiness dominates nose and taste, yet the taste is nicely balanced between the sweetness of the alcohol and the bitterness of the hop; a bone-dry degustation beer, very refreshing

FOOD PAIRING ideal with grilled sardines

Avec les bons vœux 9,5% vol. alc.

BREWED BY Brasserie Dupont, Tourpes

STYLE saison

BEN'S TASTING NOTES slightly acidic and bitter aroma; the taste is velvet soft and full in the mouth; with a herbal and bitter finish

FOOD PAIRING piquant and spicy dishes, also good with mature cheese (e.g. Stilton)

SATAN RED REGIONAL BEER

In the wake of Duvel's success a large number of strong blond beers came on the market with devilish names. Michael Jackson called them 'wicked beers' in his book. For instance, Brouwerij De Block in Peizegem, Brabant, brewed its *Satan Gold*, but for this book we tried the red version, *Satan Red*, which is intended more for export. *Satan Red* has turned out rather stronger than *Kastaar*, the best known beer in the region. The brewery has a very attractive museum, only open to visitors by appointment.

www.satanbeer.com

Satan Red 8% vol. alc.

BREWED BY Brouwerij De Block, Peizegem

STYLE red regional beer

BEN'S TASTING NOTES very caramelly, strong degustation beer with a fairly light bitter finish

FOOD PAIRING meatloaf with cherries

SERAFIJN CELTIC ANGEL   REGIONAL BEER

Achilles Van de Moer runs a tiny brewery, but with modern installations, in Itegem in the Campine region, close to the market. This choirmaster (hence the brand name Serafijn) has for years brewed splendid beers in his spare time, and gradually expanded his small brewery in his house until, to put it in Michael Jackson's words, 'the brewery consumed the house'. I remember that Mrs Van de Moer was not amused by it. By now his house has been totally absorbed, because Achilles has transformed the living room and garden into a tavern, so that the whole family eventually had to move house. The beer that impressed Michel Jackson most was the *Celtic Angel*, an Irish red ale which Achilles once brewed when he had a Scottish choir visiting him.

Serafijn Celtic Angel 6,2% vol. alc.

BREWED BY	Brouwerij Achilles, Itegem
STYLE	red regional beer
BEN'S TASTING NOTES	fairly dry beer with a trace of orange and a toasty taste of toasted malt
FOOD PAIRING	Flemish carbonade

ST. BERNARDUS ABT ABBEY BEER

In the West-Flemish village of Watou – not far from Poperinghe and known for its annual poetry event in the summer – there is yet another brewery in the Trappistenweg: St Bernardus, formerly called St Sixtus. The brewery lies secluded on a magnificent estate with a villa, which is now used for bed and breakfast. You can stay there very comfortably for several nights and let yourself be spoilt by Bernadette, wife of Guy Claus, the brewer. Behind the brewery walls brewing goes on steadily, since the beer is very successful, particularly abroad. Before 1992 it was only brewed for Westvleteren, but from that year on the monks again stoked the fires under the kettles themselves, and their beer has since blossomed into a true myth – all this despite the fathers, who would have liked to have seen things happen otherwise. They like peace and tranquillity and do everything themselves; the 6,000 hectolitres they nevertheless produce is only a fraction of the demand, which is even more stimulated by silly websites across the

world and even more foolish articles. So it is almost impossible to find the beer. And if you do find it, you pay extortionate prices. Why not, in that case, travel to St Bernardus yourself? They still brew there using the old recipes and the beers are just as good, if not better, than those of Westvleteren. As my father always said: 'why stand in a queue for hours for a beer you can get quickly just a few kilometres away?' The *St Bernardus Abt* is the strongest beer in the range, and during our tests for *Beer Passion* we called it the Rolls Royce of dark abbey beers.

St. Bernardus Abt 10% vol. alc.

BREWED BY	Brouwerij St. Bernardus, Watou
STYLE	dark abbey beer
BEN'S TASTING NOTES	aroma of green banana, fruity and slightly sweet; rich taste with fruity touches in which the CO_2 tickles the palate; a piquant, creamy beer with a fairly bitter finish
FOOD PAIRING	(daring!) sole with tarragon and creamy Noilly Prat sauce

ST. FEUILLIEN TRIPLE   ABBEY BEER

The St Feuillien brewery in the small Hainault town of Le Roeulx is 100 per cent a family business, run by Benôit and his sister, Dominique Friart. This family has been brewing beer since 1860, with a short interruption between 1980 and 1988. The *St Feuillien Triple* is the pride of the brewery, and following good Walloon tradition is full of herbs. The name comes from the Irish monk St Foillan, founder of the settlement which is the present-day town of Le Roeulx, and which had an abbey until the French revolution.

St Feuillien, like every other self-respecting abbey beer, has a blond and a brown version, which are available in a range of large bottles, from 75 cl, 1.5 litre, 3 litres, even up to 5 litres. Walloon brewing skills at their best!

St. Feuillien Triple 8,5% vol. alc.

BREWED BY Brouwerij St. Feuillien, Le Roeulx

STYLE triple abbey beer

BEN'S TASTING NOTES strong, fruity and floral nose with hints of honey and orange peel; these aromas also come out in the taste

FOOD PAIRING cod in creamy herb sauce

TIMMERMANS CAVEAU OUDE GEUZE

SPONTANEOUS FERMENTATION

Timmermans brewery in Itterbeek is perhaps the most beautiful of all lambic breweries. At the moment it is working flat out thanks to the craze for fruit beers. In 1993, when the brewery was taken over by John Martin, the chairman, Anthony Martin, immediately saw the importance of this market. He invested heavily in brewing equipment and launched numerous new fruit tastes, of which the most recent is Timmermans forest fruits. It is to his credit that in the marketing excitement about fruit beer he has yet remained faithful to the old geuze, which he has named 'caveau'. This is perhaps the most attractive of the old geuzes; it is less sour and has that whiff of fresh cedar which marks all the Timmermans beers.

Timmermans Geuze Caveau 5,5% vol. alc.

BREWED BY	Brouwerij Timmermans, Itterbeek
STYLE	old geuze
BEN'S TASTING NOTES	green fruit in the nose; soft and malty in the mouth; with a very dry, sharp and refreshing finish
FOOD PAIRING	smoked salmon, Herve cheese and the classic 'cottage cheese with radishes' from the Payotten region

TONGERLO TRIPEL BLOND   ABBEY BEER

The Norbertine abbey of Tongerlo, lying between Antwerp and Hasselt, is famous for its magnificent copy of Leonardo da Vinci's *Last Supper*. The abbey also possesses a lovely church and a well-stocked library, and many a student has taken tutorials there or gone there to cram for exams, as has your humble servant, who stayed there several days in the 1960s for tutorials during his secondary education. The Haacht brewery in Boortmeerbeek at first had the Tongerlo beers brewed elsewhere, but they gradually gained experience in brewing top fermentation beers, so that for many years the Tongerlo range (double brown, double blond and triple blond) has come from the Haacht brew-kettles too. The brewery has more than 5,000 cafés and likes to distribute its own products, because that produces most profit. The Tongerlo beers are well made; you will not find them very quickly outside the Haacht cafés, but they are well worth the discovery when you do.

Tongerlo Tripel Blond 8% vol. alc.

BREWED BY	Brouwerij Haacht, Boortmeerbeek
STYLE	triple abbey beer
BEN'S TASTING NOTES	fairly sourish nose with plenty of herbs (coriander); very herbal taste of hops with a lot of bitterness in the finish
FOOD PAIRING	risotto

TRIPEL KARMELIET ABBEY BEER

When in 1997 I went round with Michael Jackson to update his book on Great Belgian Beers, we were entertained by the Bosteels family in Buggenhout. Father Ivo and his son, Antoine Bosteels then had us taste their new beer, the Tripel Karmeliet. Everyone can remember their first Duvel, their first Orval… and equally my first Tripel Karmeliet was a real taste sensation.

Antoine Bosteels had found an old recipe based on three grains: barley, wheat and oats, in the library of the Carmelite monastery in Dendermonde. This recipe lay behind Bosteel's decision to brew a triple with 8 per cent of alcohol, something which they had not previously had in their range.

Bosteels was then best known for their *Kwak*, an amber-coloured beer served in the famous glass with the wooden stand. Bosteels saw prospects for a multigrain beer and developed one, and young Antoine designed the splendid label with the Carmelite brothers threshing, as well as the famous tall goblet with the stylized fleur-de-lis burnt into it. The beer became a success quite quickly and today serves as a reference in the field of triples, although some connoisseurs find it a little on the sweet side. In any case, it is one of the leaders at the annual *Beer Passion Weekend* in Antwerp.

Tripel Karmeliet 8% vol. alc.

BREWED BY	Brouwerij Bosteels, Buggenhout
STYLE	triple abbey beer
BEN'S TASTING NOTES	fruit (peach, apricot) and cloves in the nose; the taste is soft, tending towards sweet, yet the beer is still refreshing and very drinkable
FOOD PAIRING	sole with a cream sauce

Tripel Karmeliet

WESTMALLE TRIPEL TRAPPIST

Beer has been brewed in the Trappist abbey at Westmalle since 1794. Beer brewing here prides itself on a tradition that states that, according to St Benedict's monastic rules, the monks should provide as much as possible of their own necessities of life, and moreover, should entertain guests and visitors properly with drinks from their own region. To play safe, we'd better make that regional beverage ourselves, they must have thought. The beauty of this abbey beer is that the monks strive for as high a quality as possible and use modern brewing methods, while following centuries-old traditions. Pure well water from Westmalle, genuine hops, malt and yeast are the only ingredients.

As well as the dark *Westmalle Dubbel*, the brothers brew a delightful triple, which in recent years has gone to the top of the sales figures. It first saw the light in 1937, to the recipe of Henri Verlinden, master brewer of the Witkap Brewery in Brasschaat and adviser to

---

Westmalle Tripel 9,5% vol. alc.

BREWED BY Onze-Lieve-Vrouwe-abdij (Abbey of Our Lady), Westmalle

STYLE triple trappist beer

BEN'S TASTING NOTES golden blond; aroma of fruit (overripe banana), together with a maltiness and a fine bitterness; this beer is delicately sweet in the mouth without being cloying; the finish is pleasantly bitter

FOOD PAIRING ideal with Flemish asparagus

the brothers. *Westmalle Tripel* is the mother of all the triples in the world, its taste is unequalled, and the problem is that after drinking a *Westmalle Tripel* you find it difficult to drink any other beer. It is clear why Michael Jackson called the beer 'a world classic'.

Westmalle Dubbel 6,5% vol. alc.

BREWED BY Onze-Lieve-Vrouwe-abdij (Abbey of Our Lady), Westmalle

STYLE dark trappist beer

BEN'S TASTING NOTES soft feel in the mouth, malt and coffee on the palate, which, thanks to some aniseed and passion fruit ends up in a dry finsh

FOOD PAIRING live the life of Riley: serve with fresh brown bread and some abbey cheese

WITTEKERKE ROSÉ WHITE BEER

Wittekerke is the name of a recently defunct soap on VTM (Flemish television). But Wittekerke also became the name of a white (wheat) beer when in 1998, as a marketing consultant, I was able to persuade VTM and Bavik brewery to use the name for a brand of white beer. That was all to the brewery's benefit, since the name was widely familiar from the TV programme. However, the market for white beer collapsed, but fortunately they managed to turn the tide with a new creation: a raspberry beer based on Wittekerke. The idea of calling the beer *Rosé* actually came from Michael Jackson. I had suggested it earlier to Rodenbach, but they saw nothing in it and turned it down. Bavik took it up, launched their beer under the name Wittekerke Rosé, and cast their eyes mainly at the Netherlands, pre-eminently the rosé wine market. It went so well that Heineken too, and later Inbev, also came on the market with a 'rosé' white beer.

Wittekerke Rosé 5% vol. alc.

BREWED BY Brouwerij Bavik, Bavikhove (Harelbeke)

STYLE rosé white beer

BEN'S TASTING NOTES this beer is sweet, but thanks to the slight sourness of the old brown in it (Petrus), it is still easy to drink and refreshing, but it should be served ice-cold

FOOD PAIRING ideal with sweet desserts, also good in a zabaglione, which it makes a pretty pink colour

BELGIAN
BEER
SOMMELIER

INDEX

A

Abbaye des Rocs 23, 55
abbey beer 22
Achel Blond 56
Achel Extra Bruin 59
adjuncts 30
Adriaen Brouwer 61
Affligem Blond 62
aperitif 163
asparagus 85, 179
Augustijn 65
Avec les bons voeux 163

B

barley 30
beer sommelier 16, 45, 47
blue cheese 79
boiling 30, 37
'*bolleke*' 87
Boon Oude Kriek 66
Bornem Tripel 69
bouillabaisse 69, 117
Brugge Tripel 73
Brugse Zot 76
Bush Grand Prestige 79

C

caramel malt 30
carbon dioxide 29, 31, 38, 39
carbonade 61, 166
cassoulet 105
catfish 73, 80
ceviche 97, 130, 159
cheese 136, 160, 163
cherries 126, 138, 139, 165
cherry 26, 27, 30, 66, 126, 138
chicory with ham 143
Chimay Cinq Cents 80
Chimay Grande Réserve 83
chocolate 61, 83, 97
chocolate gateau 52, 110
Cistercians 22, 56
cod 170
cooling 37
coriander 31
cork 45
corn 30
Corsendonk Agnus 85
Corsendonk Pater 85
curaçao 31

D

De Koninck 87
deglaze 51
dégorgement 26, 109, 131
Delirium Tremens 88
Deus Brut des Flandres 90
dishes, oriental 153
dishes, spicy 163
Double Enghien 93
draff 37
Drie Fonteinen Oude Geuze 94
Duchesse de Bourgogne 96
Duvel 98

Index

E

eel 147
Ename Tripel 101
enzymes 30, 34
escabeche 97, 159

F

fermentation, bottom 11, 34, 39
fermentation, mixed 26, 31
fermentation, spontaneous 26, 31
fermentation, top 19, 31
filtration 37, 38
fish 74, 107
'foeders' (tuns) 94, 157, 158
food pairing 51
fruit beer 27, 34

G

game 55
geuze 26, 66, 94, 130, 173
goat's cheese 51, 125
Gouden Carolus Classic 102, 105
Gouden Carolus Triple 105
goulash 110
grain 29, 30
Grimbergen Blond 107
Grimbergen Cuvée de l'Ermitage 22
Grottenbier 109
Gulden Draak 110

H

Hapkin 112
Havana cigar 59, 83, 137
head 47
head of foam 46
herbs and spices 154
herring 97
Hoegaarden 115

hop 30
hotpot 93

K

Kasteel Bruin 117
Kasteel Tripel 117
Keizer Karel Ruby Red 119
kriek (cherry) 26, 27, 30, 66, 126, 138

L

La Chouffe 120
lager (mature) 38
lamb cutlets 137
lambic 26, 27, 30, 31, 66, 94, 130
lay brewer 59
Leffe Blond 123
Liefmans Gouden Band 125
Liefmans Kriek 126
Lindemans Cuvée René 129, 130
liquorice 31
lobster 73, 117

M

Malheur 10 135
Malheur Brut Réserve 131
malt 30, 31, 34, 37, 46
malt, pale 30
malt, toasted 30, 125
Maredsous 8 136, 137
Maredsous Tripel 137
mash 34
maturation 26
mature 38
maturing 19
meat loaf 126
meat loaf 165
méthode champenoise 26
Michael Jackson 15

mixing beer 38
Moinette Blonde 163
monkfish 71
Mort Subite Oude Kriek 138
mussels 94

O
oast 30
Orval 140
ox cheek 137
oysters 91

P
Palm Royale 144
Palm Spéciale 143
partridge 73, 154
pasta carbonara 88
pasteurize 189
paté de campagne 65
Pater Lieven Blond 147
Pauwel Kwak 148
Petrus Gouden Tripel 150
pils 19, 31
pils malt 30, 98
Pilsner Urquell 19
Poperings Hommelbier 153
pork 105
pouring 45, 46
prawns 99, 130, 158, 159
pure cultures 19

Q
quail 73

R
rabbit 73, 105
regional beer 23
rémuage 26, 109, 131

risotto 174
Rodenbach 157
Rodenbach Grand Cru 159

S
Saison Dupont 161
saisons 25, 74, 93, 160, 163
salad 51
salmon 62, 88, 115, 150, 173
sardines 115, 163
Satan Red 165
saturate 38
scampi 76, 144
second fermentation 19, 30, 38, 39
Serafijn Celtic Angel 166
sniff 48
sole 47, 91, 93, 99, 125
sole, fillets of 151
spare ribs 137
special beers 51, 88, 102, 109, 143
spéciale belge 25, 87, 143, 144
squid 105
St Bernardus Abt 169
St Feuillien Triple 170
steak 52, 85, 113
sterilization 37
stew 109
Straffe Hendrik 74, 76
styles of beer 19
sugar 30, 37, 38, 39
sugar, conversion to 34

T
tannin 66
terroir 23, 55
Timmermans Geuze Caveau 173
Tongerlo Tripel blond 174
Trappist 22, 34, 52

Index

Trappist monastery 22, 140
Tripel Karmeliet 149, 176, 177
triple 69, 73, 101, 116, 150, 174, 176, 179
tuna 56, 133
tuna steak 123
tuns 94, 157, 158
turbot 115

W

Westmalle Dubbel 179, 180
Westmalle Tripel 179
wheat 30
white (wheat) beer 25
Wittekerke Rosé 183

Y

yeast 19, 29, 31, 34, 37
yeast sediment 39

Z

zabaglione 126, 130, 183

www.lannoo.com

Lannoo Publishers
Kasteelstraat 97, B-8700 Tielt
lannoo@lannoo.be
Postbus 614, NL-6800 AP Arnhem
info@terralannoo.nl

Text: Ben Vinken
Text 'How is beer made?: Jef Van den Steen
Photography: Joris Luyten
Layout: Keppie & Keppie
English translation: Alastair and Cora Weir
With thanks to O'COOL for the material for the photo shoot

Printed and bound by Drukkerij Die Keure, Bruges, 2008

© Uitgeverij Lannoo nv, Tielt, 2008
ISBN 978 90 209 7920 6 • NUR 440 • D/2008/45/304

All rights reserved. No part of this book may be reproduced, stored in a retrieval system, or transmitted in any form or by any means, electronic, electrostatic, magnetic tape, mechanical, photocopying, recording or otherwise, without the prior permission in writing of the publisher.